THE ANGEL LETTERS

THE
$\mathcal{A}$NGEL
LETTERS

Lessons That Dying Can Teach Us About Living

———

Norman J. Fried, Ph.D.

IVAN R. DEE · CHICAGO

Quotations from *Goodnight Moon* are used by permission of HarperCollins Publishers. *Goodnight Moon* © 1947 by Harper & Row. Text © renewed 1975 by Roberta Brown Rauch. Illustrations © renewed 1975 by Edith Hurd, Clement Hurd, John Thacher Hurd, and George Hellyer, as Trustees of the Edith & Clement Hurd 1982 Trust.

Library of Congress Cataloging-in-Publication Data:
Fried, Norman J.
    The angel letters : lessons that dying can teach us about living / Norman J. Fried.
        p. cm.
    Includes index.
    ISBN-13: 978-1-56663-718-3 (cloth : alk. paper)
    ISBN-10: 1-56663-718-X (cloth : alk. paper)
  1. Terminally ill children—Miscellanea. 2. Death—Miscellanea.
3. Dying—Miscellanea. I. Title.
    RJ249.F752 2006
    155.9'37—dc22

                                                    2006022193

For my father, David H. Fried,

and for Gregg Saberito, my friend through the ages

Contents

Foreword

THE SWEETEST LESSONS are sometimes learned through bitterness and pain. And the scenes of our lives, when viewed through the loving eyes of strangers and friends, can teach us so much about ourselves no matter how painful the message. These are my thoughts as I introduce you to the children in this book. For during the course of my years working with pediatric oncology patients, I have viewed many scenes from life and have come to learn much about its true challenges. I have been sadly fortunate to sit at the bedsides of children with life-threatening illnesses. I have listened carefully as they shared their messages of hope and love, and taught me how to help those they were leaving behind. It has been years since I looked into the eyes of many of these children. Looking into the past, it is their eyes that I remember most—how they glistened with hope and gratitude, how they spoke wordlessly and told me what they urgently needed me to know. The children you will read about here had so much to teach; it is these lessons, "messages for the living," that I hope to convey to you in this book.

As a psychotherapist and counselor to both the physically ill and the worried well, I am struck by the paradox of living—how we go about our lives, gloriously unaware of our vulnerability, until one day, without warning, the telephone rings, a doctor enters a consulting room, or a newspaper headline calls out. Then without regret for what it sweeps away, life ushers us into a new world. We quickly learn that the person we were only moments ago is changed forever. And we are lost.

It is mourners who have taught me about living after a death. As mourners, we cry out loud. We pound our chests and rail against our fate. We ask God for mercy even as we know we have been refused. Mortality, whose graven touch we long to escape, reaches out to us. Words like "hope" and "faith" seem foreign now, meaningful only to the naive and the unafflicted.

We discover that we are unaware of the passage of time. Loved ones and friends go on with their lives; everyone around us continues to change and grow. But our own lives have frozen in time, as if everything moves around us while we stand still, trapped in memory and loss.

We learn that even the process of our own aging eludes us. We lose all references to milestones and "age markers." We merely get through, enduring one day at a time. The future ceases to exist.

We learn that men and women grieve differently. As women who mourn, we surrender totally to grief, allowing it to invade every part of our being. We become our grief. By giving in to the pain, we adapt to every new step we take. As a person who is suddenly stricken lame must accept the fact that she can no longer walk, we learn that something utterly foreign is required of us just to get from one place to another.

Men, on the other hand, believe that in order to survive they must function. Many men fear that giving in to grief will cause them to implode, to deteriorate, never again to be the person they once were. As men who mourn, we go to work and engage in the tasks of the living—we pay the bills and fill the car with gas. But we are not truly present. We simply go through the motions and realize that others heal in ways that we cannot. We become hollow.

I have learned from mourners how friends speak of hopeful things: "He is in a better place," they say. They smile and assert that "God gives us only as much as we can handle." But we know that these expressions of support are vain attempts to ease the pain. To the broken-hearted they are empty words—mixtures of meaningless syllables more likely to soothe the soul of the speaker than the soul of the mourner. We may apply words as one would a balm or salve on a wound that we hope will heal in time. But grief respects no such cure. Words rarely penetrate the souls of the broken and despairing.

How then do we survive the pain of loss? How do we make sense of tragedy, sickness, and suffering? And what are the lessons, if any, to be learned from our mortal, human journey? Preachers speak of God and await His return. Mothers of ill children speak of shattered dreams; they pray for healing and await their nightmare's end. Children speak of separation and sadness, and wait in vain for their loved one to come home.

This book is my attempt to wrestle with these questions. It is the culmination of lessons learned during fifteen years of work in the pediatric oncology center of a hospital in New York. It is comprised of letters and essays about the children I grew to know and dearly love as they battled with end-stage cancer and life-threatening blood disorders. The letters, though elegiac, are meant to be stories of everyday heroes and teachers. The postscripts that follow the letters are offered as my own interpretations of the messages that each child's death conveys to us, the living. Little has been altered save names; what is written here is essentially true.

No story ends in death—not in this book, and not in life. What happens after death is ours to ponder and struggle with.

Does a heaven await us? Are we met by the warm, mystical light of God or by the outstretched arms of a loved one who departed long ago? Or do we simply cease to breathe and end our biological functioning only to return to the earth? These questions remain unanswered; for what awaits us after dark, divine or otherwise, is not for us to know. But how a family lives after a death, how we as mourners can carry on—these are the questions I wrestle with here.

Through poetry, metaphor, and storytelling, children revealed their secrets, their fears, and their awareness of death to me. Through their friendship, their need for parenting and prayer, they taught me how to help their loved ones say the necessary words of goodbye. It has been said that dying children speak in metaphor and symbolism. I believe this is true. As the letters and essays that follow reveal, the symbols and wishes at the end of life make our dying livable and our living worth dying for.

Acknowledgments

The Angel Letters represents the culmination of years of effort by many dear friends, colleagues, teachers, and patients. In particular, the work involved in the care of the children who are the subjects of these letters is integrally connected to the excellent attention each child received by the medical and psychosocial staff at the Cancer Center for Kids at Winthrop University Hospital and the Children's Cancer Center of North Shore University Hospital in New York. For fifteen years I have had the honor to work with Dr. Mark Weinblatt and Dr. Philip Scimeca and their staff of doctors, nurses, psychologists, social workers, and child-life specialists, and together we created a medical environment where very sick children can heal.

The theories I offer in this book reflect the integration of study and practice inspired by many great thinkers in the disciplines of psychology, philosophy, and literature. In particular, interested readers are referred to the existential writings of Irvin Yalom, Erich Fromm, Rainer Maria Rilke, and Viktor Frankl. In addition, the spiritual theories of Carl Jung, Clarissa Pinkola Estes, and Larry Dossey are referred to in several chapters, as are the psychological writings of Earl Grollman, Sandra Sutherland Fox, and

Beverly James. The intergenerational interpretations used in "A Lesson in Truth" have been gleaned from the seminal works of Murray Bowen and Maggie Scarf. The technique of narrative psychotherapy utilized in "A Lesson in Strength" was inspired by the writings of David Epston, and the use of corresponding narrative and subnarrative dialogues in "A Lesson in Love" was inspired by John Berger. The poetry of E. M. Cioran and the prose of Jonathan Carroll, as well as the timeless words of Margaret Wise Brown, are also gratefully acknowledged.

I wish to acknowledge Debbie Goldman, a friend and colleague who read and reread the many versions of *The Angel Letters* as they were being written, and who supported me through the process.

Bobby Dor, my friend, spent countless hours reading the letters and discussing their significance to her own life. Her words and emotions meant much to me; they served as the catalyst for the postscripts, or clinical essays, that follow each letter. I am grateful, also, to Benny Dor, a man I never met, but whose spirit is represented throughout much of the text that follows.

Barbara Weinblatt deserves special recognition. I thank her for the time she spent reading and editing the letters and essays.

The following people offered their support and advice during the writing and publishing of this book: Scott Fried; Arthur Kurzweil; Dale, James, Matthew, and Geralyn Hisiger; Sharon Coritsidis, CPNP, CPON; Dr. Renee Exelbert; Dr. Nira Golombeck; Dr. Jerry Kleiman; Nancy Barbach, LCSW; Marianne Bidell; and Susan Jacobson. I am grateful to each of them for their ideas, for their wisdom, and for their love.

I wish to acknowledge my mother, Selma Fried, who, through love and tears, taught me about the true power of healing.

My wife Beth and my sons Joshua, Jacob, and David are the motivation and force behind everything I do. I honor them here as I do every day.

Finally, I wish to thank Ivan Dee, who liked the possibilities of *The Angel Letters* enough to publish it.

N. J. F.

Manhasset, New York
October 2006

*Who, if I cried out, would hear me among the angels'
hierarchies? And even if one of them pressed me
suddenly against his heart I would be consumed in
that overwhelmong existence. For beauty is nothing but
the beginning of terror, which we still are just able to endure.*

—*Rainer Maria Rilke, The Duino Elegies*

THE ANGEL LETTERS

I

A Lesson in Friendship

To live is to build a ship and a harbor at the same time
And to complete the harbor long after the ship has sunk.
—Yehudah Amichai

D ear Emily,

Today marks two years since your death. I realize now that as time passes it gets harder, not easier. I keep your picture on the desk in my office. It sits in the frame attached to a picture of the Power Puff Girls, favorite cartoon characters of yours. Children ask me all the time: Is that your sister? Is that your wife? "No," I answer. "She's my friend." Because the truth is, I never felt like a therapist who provided you with guidance or support. I always thought of myself as a friend who came by the bone marrow unit to hang out with you and help you pass the time. And as your time in the unit wore on, so did your stories of your high school years, and of your friends and the fun times you had with them. We gossiped about the nurses you liked and the nurses you didn't; about the latest annoying thing that the social worker had said to you; and about your plans for your life after your discharge from the hospital. Together we traveled back in time to your childhood, then fantasized in fast forward about your bright future. And so it was, in that casual way of yours, that you allowed me to help you endure your journey through cancer.

You were always so afraid of the bone marrow unit. You wanted to be sure to be out and back at home in time for the prom. It was your senior year in high school, a year of new beginnings and so many endings. And when you did not make it to the prom, you said it was okay with you. And when you did not want your friends to tell you about it and they came anyway, and told you their stories of who wore what and who danced with whom, still you listened, smiling. It was always okay as long as your friends were happy.

You were in the hospital the day the yearbook came out. Your mom brought it in for you to look at while you rested and tried to get better. I was so excited for you, and I was glad to finally attach faces to all of the names we had spoken about for weeks. I remember coming in the next day with my old yearbook. I showed you my senior photo, and you told me that I "must have been a 'hottie' back in high school." It's funny, Emily. I don't remember myself in the way you saw me in that picture. Maybe you were right, maybe I was "cool," as you put it. "Cool" was your word for so many things. I couldn't attend your family's fund-raising event at the Knights of Columbus hall, an event that would help defray the costs of your bone marrow transplant. But that was "cool" with you. The doctors couldn't keep their promise to get you home in time for the prom. But that, too, was "cool."

The truth is, you were cool, Emily. The word, its sound and form, defined you. You were a young lady with the heart and soul of a little girl. You drew silly pictures with your girlfriends, and made a sign for your door that said "No Therapists Allowed," at the same time you dealt bravely with life and death and waited day after day for reports of your recovery. You spoke of the funny videos that you and your friend made in the kitchen at home on rainy days, then talked about the Cabriolet convertible that your dad would have waiting for you upon your discharge from the hospital. These were some of the contradictions in your treacherous journey, one you undertook so courageously and often in great pain. Yes, Emily, you were definitely cool.

It was one week before graduation when your oncologist went to Europe on a vacation. She said she would see you when she returned, and she transferred your care to her associate. I remember sitting in the office of the chief of oncology with your mother and father and an assistant psychologist that afternoon, talking about the options you had. Your father wanted another medical opinion. He was losing faith in the doctors. He thought the slowdown in your kidney function was a bad sign. The doctors had told him that they were exploring all options, but that each of them posed complications. If they gave you one medicine, it might help your cell count but hurt your kidneys. Without it, your kidney function might improve, but what about your blood count? Would it improve on its own? Back and forth your father raged against these choices and against the doctors who gave him information that changed with every passing day, while your mother silently raged against your father for realizing so late how dire your situation truly was. Her hurt was based in his extreme commitment to his job and his ever-positive attitude toward your illness. But there, in the green glow of the chief's small desk lamp, they came to a mutual decision.

Because you were almost eighteen years old and your muscular athletic body was more a woman's than a child's, you would be transferred to the division of adult medicine. New hope was breathed into those stale days. Your mother and father cautiously but openly rejoiced that they had finally found the right doctors, the right medical setting. You would finally get better. You would be treated by specialists trained in the care of adult bone marrow transplantation and kidney function.

The adult unit was indeed more of a comprehensive care setting. As before, you had your own room, but visitors were strictly forbidden, other than your mother, your father, and your older brother Jack. And the doctors, of course. So I became a doctor again, Emily. I ceased being your "friend" to hang with and gossip about your day, and became instead a psychologist with official permission to help you smile.

You slept most of the time, a side effect of the pain medicine you were given. Were you aware of our presence? Did you feel our warm wishes of hope and love? Did you know about the world outside your door? The glass wall that separated you from infection and recontamination, from the air we breathe daily for our own sustenance, was kept shut at all times. The curtains you always wanted closed "for privacy from therapists" were also secured. We sat outside day after day. When a doctor went in to check your vital signs, we said prayers and blew kisses through the momentary opening in the wall.

The doctors informed your mother that you were not getting better. She was told daily that your body was becoming toxified by the buildup of uric acid in your system. Finally, the day came when your mother was told to gather your family and friends in order to say goodbye. She sat with you for a while, then left to say her good-byes at the home where you had lived. She spent the remainder of the day in your living room with your family and your best girl-friends. Your father held a vigil outside those glass doors. I re-member how I found him there, lost and confused. All of your life he had had the answers for you whenever you were in need. But on this day he sat stupefied, watching as doctors came and went from your room. Some he had never seen before. Some he had come to know well. Their faces blank and unreadable, they passed like ac-tors entering and exiting a scene in a play. We were not allowed to go backstage to meet them to learn what was truly happening.

We sat there that way for hours, waiting. I thought of how similar this was to the waiting rooms of maternity wards: fathers and friends waiting impatiently for a soul's arrival into a new and different world. Your father cried as he recalled the wonderful days of your childhood. You were his favorite, Emily. And I could see why as I came to know him better—you were two eternal opti-mists, and you both found ways to laugh through life. As we sat to-gether, he began to question his faith, his God, his own choices and decisions. He asked me if I thought he was being punished for something he had done in his youth. He asked me why the doctors wouldn't talk to us as they passed. He told me how your eyes no longer responded when he looked into them. He knew you were leaving, Emily, and he agonized over his decision not to sign the Do Not Resuscitate order. How could he put his signature to a form that would end all chances to bring you back?

Finally, the chief of the medical intensive care unit came over and explained that you had "coded." Doctors and nurses from all over the hospital rushed into your room to perform the acts nec-essary to save your life. When the chief told your father that these procedures would be more invasive than lifesaving, your father asked for my opinion. I stood in silence for a moment, then reminded him of his own words—that you were "leaving." He told the doctors to stop all procedures, to simply let you be. And they agreed.

He asked to be with you one last time, and was granted his wish. The nurses prepared you so that your dad could hold you as you drew your last breaths. He held you and whispered in your ear, as you left him, as you left us all.

And in a few moments he was gone—down the hall, without you.

This part of the story you may not know. I sat there alone at your door, thinking of you and of our friendship, of your mother and father, and of all that you had just left behind. The very next day you would have graduated from high school and attended the commencement ceremony marking the next phase of your life. I thought about how you never got to ride in that Cabriolet. I realized you would never throw your cap high up in the air or turn your tassel to the right. Or is it the left? No matter now. Did you ever drink a beer or kiss a boy? Did you ever say the parting words that you longed for your friends and family to hear? I wondered these things as I realized that I now lived in a world without your presence, your jokes, your grace.

As I went to the nurses' station to call home, I noticed one of your friends, frightened and crying in a corner. When I approached her and asked how long she had been there, she replied, "All day." She said she did not want to interfere with your family's grief and had sat quietly watching from afar. I told her that you had just died and that your father was with you, and that your mother was at home with the rest of your friends. I asked her if she wanted to sit by your door for a few moments to have a chance to say goodbye. So we sat together by the slight opening in the glass that your father had left when he turned away from you. I told her that I would sit outside your door until the nurses prepared your body to be taken away. She thanked me and called her mother to take her home. What a strange irony.

I visited your family several times that summer. Pulling up to your house I would find your mother and father sitting in silence under the carport, staring at the flickering light of the television. Your father took me on long vigorous walks during which he talked about possible mistakes the doctors had made in your care. His grief for you manifested itself through anger and demands for action, whether destructive or constructive. Your mother, on the other hand, sat quietly with me under that carport and indulged in memories of you. She enjoyed these visits, and I had a strong desire to know more about the young woman you had been before you became ill. Sometimes your friends came by and we talked about the fun you used to have together. Your mother always showed so much compassion for them and so much interest in their lives. Michelle was off to Spain for the summer; Sarah was getting ready for college in the fall. Your mom lived through their journeys and was fortified by stories of you that she had never heard before, stories that only girlfriends can tell.

But she was breaking inside and losing interest in summoning the energy to smile. She would not go into the house at all that summer, except to sleep. She told me it was too painful to be inside, that as long as the weather held, there she would stay. Maybe she was holding a vigil until you came home. Or maybe she believed the house would never truly feel like home again.

When winter came, your mom and I agreed to meet in my private office. She needed to speak about you, to wrap herself in her grief and her longing for you. We sat, hour after hour, calling up memories that she was afraid would someday grow pale and distant. Hour after hour she spoke of the "what ifs," as she called them: What if we had gone to Seattle for the transplant? They were the best—what if they could have saved her? What if we had kept her in the pediatric unit and not with the adult patients? What if we had followed a different plan? Your mother was consumed by her sorrow and by her need to answer these questions, and yet she longed to end her obsession. Moreover she needed to understand why she could not relinquish the "what if" thought process.

I told her that for all your life she had asked herself "what if" questions: What if you forgot to bring a warm coat to school on a cold day? What if you didn't have enough money in your pocket? What if you were scared and needed her? I told her that I did not think she was ready to stop being your mother simply because you had died—that by continuing to ask the "what if" questions, she continued to act as your caretaker and worrier. I reminded her of what she had once told me—that being your mother was the only job she ever wanted and was the best job she ever had. I told her that she was not ready to give up that role because it defined her and kept her whole. She was not yet capable of ending her role as your mother. She was not ready to let you go.

All that winter your mother buried herself in art projects and anger. Her anger seemed to propel her creativity, for she produced many beautiful pieces. One was a montage of her view of the world after the September 11 attacks on the World Trade Center. We spoke of how she might constructively turn her talents and her pain into a means of making money. And she started a small business painting decorative designs and murals on the walls of her neighbors' houses. She told me how this activity afforded her many hours of solitude and solace. She made every brush stroke with you in mind. There were no distractions, no small talk, just pure time alone with her art and her grief. I believe this helped your mother stay connected to you and contribute in her own small way to the outside world she had come to know only from afar.

The anniversary of your death approached, and your mother did not know how to honor the day. She didn't even know if acknowledging it was possible. She spoke of how painful the anticipation of that day was becoming. As June 27 drew nearer, she found herself less settled, less at peace with the world. She struggled with the idea of gathering your friends for a memorial, or of sitting quietly with your father and brother, or of spending the day alone with a memory box filled with mementoes of you. Finally, at the last moment, she settled on the idea of a bonfire, and she invited everyone she could think of to attend in your honor.

I drove to your house on that anniversary day, and there on the lawn was a festival of you. All of your girlfriends, now one year into their college experiences, sat around tables and on benches, drinking beer and listening to your favorite Dave Matthews CDs. Michelle was back from Spain; your relatives were there; your little cousins threw beach balls and laughed; Jack, your brother, came with his new girlfriend. And everyone brought a note or letter written for you. One by one, they walked up to a great cast-iron furnace sitting in the center of your driveway and offered their letters of love to the fire. I wonder, did you ever receive those letters, Emily? Did you know that we were all there, loving you and celebrating your life?

And so today, as another anniversary of your passing is marked, I have written another letter to you. Even in death, you continue to teach, for I am learning still about myself and my place in the world of the bereaved. And here is the lesson that hurts most. A few weeks after the bonfire in your honor, I had to leave town without notice and I called your mother long-distance to cancel our meeting for that week. I told her that we would reschedule upon my return. But I never called her again, and I did not hear from her either. As time wore on, I found myself caught in a current of strange and conflicting emotions. What stopped me from calling? Had I become too close to your family? Was I losing my ability to see your mother's pain objectively? Was I burning out? Something inside of me was hurt by my meetings with your mother, and perhaps I thought that ending our meetings would preserve me.

I had become your friend, Emily. And maybe your mother made me her friend too. Maybe she was unsure about reconnecting for fear that it would hurt too much to be with your friends in this painful time. Maybe she expected more from me than my role and my heart allowed. And I realize now that emotions expressed in friendship, unlike those expressed through the safer, more boundaried therapeutic relationship, can cause deep waves of personal pain. Sometimes people are swept under. I realize now that I too was swept under.

So here I am, friend, two years past your death, and still sometimes feeling mired in sadness, shame, and regret: shame that I did not set boundaries that would allow me to guide your mother and father better; regret that I do not get to hang with you anymore or visit your family. Perhaps writing this letter will bring me closer to some resolution. In writing you, I realize how very much you taught me, and I affirm that our friendship was not forged in vain. Indeed, I know now that friendship is a gift, and that we were truly gifted. And I believe that in order to heal a soul, one must be willing to love, even if loving causes us pain, regret, and sorrow.

ᔕ POSTSCRIPT

In loving we make ourselves vulnerable to the pain of loss. Grief is the currency of love, the price we pay for caring about another person. In asserting our love, we open ourselves to the world and, in return, the world gives back its lessons. It teaches us, through contradiction, that we are capable of greatness even when we feel small. Indeed it is at the times when we feel small, ashamed, abused, or "burned out" that we are being challenged to grow. When at first the world delivers crushing blows of loss and pain, we find ourselves down on the canvas with little will to get up and fight. And yet the wish to live prevails. Someday we will want to live again, as hard as that is to believe now.

As Yehudah Amichai says, we must continue to build the harbor, long after the ship has sunk. We must thus ask ourselves: What is our harbor made of? What is its essence? Is it made up only of the memories of our loved one? Indeed not, for it includes the rituals of lives lived together. It includes the places we went together, the taste of a favorite soup, the smell of her hair, or the song he loved to sing. It is the memory of his face in the doorway, his voice on the telephone saying "I love you." It consists of a glance at her picture or a look into her bedroom, untouched and unfinished. But a harbor also includes the glimmer of happiness we feel when we are caught off guard by a funny joke or a momentary wish for a pretty blouse or a fast car. For quietly lying underneath the burden of shock and pain are the parallel forces of hope and desire. And as they are revealed, so too is our strength.

Grieving, however, and the strength needed to endure our suffering, is not a linear process. It more resembles a spiral staircase on which are recapitulated earlier themes of loss, anger, disbelief, and the hope for eventual repair. We hire a painter to paint the house, or spend large sums of money on new clothes one day, only to catch ourselves saying, "I want to have a heart attack and be out of this place" the next. We feel "schizophrenic" and disconnected from the order that seems to surround everyone else. We discover that we are victims of the confluence of two forces: the instinctual will to live and the raw awareness of what life has truly done to us. Like the toddler who runs away from his parents with one eye always looking back for reassurance, we flirt with independence from our grief even as we retreat into the arms of our pain.

Friends and family rarely allow us the freedom to express our despair for fear that we mean all that we say. "My life as I know it is over!" we cry. But our friends define our healing only through our happiness. They long for our return to our earlier, "lighter" selves. "It's time to move on," they implore. "Time will help you heal." "He is in a better place." They want to "fix" what they perceive as broken, unaware that it is not their responsibility to fix us. Few understand that the person we were before loss entered our lives has changed, and forevermore. The friends among whom we once walked so comfortably, now feel more like strangers. If only they knew that we don't want to "move on." If only they would acknowledge that we *are* changed, that we *are* different. Yes, we will laugh again, but not in the same way. We will dance, and smile, and attend gatherings with friends, but inside we will always have our sadness, our private sorrow.

Thus when winter comes, and night falls early, we wrap ourselves in our grief. Nature resonates with our internal world. We are safe in our blanket of solitude, frayed and threadbare though we may be. And when springtime comes and the flowers bloom, and there is a resurrection of all that was once fallow and dormant, we feel that spring is our enemy. It mocks us, shining its rays of life when we are filled with death. Though we may feebly "whistle a happy tune," we realize that we cannot compete with the blooming symphony all around us. We discover, as one mourner described, that we are "playing 'Chopsticks' while nature is conducting Beethoven."

We learn to search for peers, fellow mourners, who understand sadness as we do. Support groups have been established and designed for the mourners among us. Some are quite helpful for they offer us a chance to speak a common language with others who are in a similar place. We can cry without being judged and laugh without being questioned. We can admit to being baffled at how the ordinary things in life—the color of a kitchen countertop or a dent in a new car—seem to matter so much to others but no longer to us. Even a trip to the emergency room to set a child's broken arm doesn't bother us, for we know that in time it will heal. We discover the difference between psychotherapy and self-help groups. In particular, groups led by experienced psychotherapists and grief counselors seem more comforting than self-help groups without skilled facilitators—we do not wish to be overexposed to the sorrows of others. It is a precarious path we travel, for while fellow mourners may listen with a more compassionate ear, we know that they also have their stories to tell. And many of us are not ready, or able, to open our hearts to their burdens.

We may find ourselves dividing the world into two categories of people—those who expect us to "get over" our pain, and the rarer ones who understand our need to "get through" it. We find solace in the presence of that one friend who understands our involuntary, and perhaps compulsive, need to journey *through* the darkness we feel. In telling our story of loss in this safe context, no matter how often, no matter how sad, we learn that we are beginning to master the trauma we have been through. For in telling our story we are simultaneously bidding farewell to our old life and defining a new one. In addition, we discover that we are being honored and understood without being minimized. Last, and without our full awareness, we are slowly carving a place in our inner psyches where this knowledge may rest. Now, instead of tripping over our grief as we journey into the next phase of life, we find a way to make it our traveling companion.

Through it all, we remain grateful. Grateful for the love we had and the life we knew when we were with our loved one. We are grateful for the wisdom their living has imparted. And we are learning to be grateful even for the lessons that in dying they are trying to teach us.

2

A Lesson in Love

*There is a land of the living and a land of the dead
and the bridge is love;
The only survival, the only meaning.*
*—Thornton Wilder,
The Bridge of San Luis Rey*

Dear Paloma,

There is a moment in life when we all are forced to learn that, even in love, we make this journey alone. This is the lesson that haunts me when I tell your story. For yours was a life filled with the desire for love and the wish to be counted as one of two. You were a sixteen-year-old girl, a junior in high school with homework and friends and dreams of the future. You met your boyfriend when you were hale and whole; you spent long days and nights with him, defying your mother and the rules of her household whenever possible. But the leukemia in your blood grew, and you and your boyfriend would soon contend with the trials of treatment, and the inevitable sorrows of hair loss and hospital stays.

I did not fully understand back then that it was love, not success, compliance, or even good health, that guided you. Instead I joined the doctors in their frustration and fury over your missed appointments, your frequent disappearances, your misplaced medicines. Your mother would come alone to the clinic on mornings when you were scheduled for chemotherapy, and await your arrival with quiet uncertainty. I realize now, looking back in time, that she understood your needs better than we thought. Indeed, it was your mother who quietly allowed you to find your own way. Rarely did she punish you for staying out night after night or for arriving late to your doctor appointments.

The social worker in the cancer center had many discussions with your mother about her need to get a "better handle" on your whereabouts, about her failed attempts at "limit setting." I see now that your mother was neither weak nor unaware. She knew what was at stake for you, and she held fast to her maternal instincts. You were a girl in love; she wanted you to have all that she knew you were about to lose. This is why she allowed you to move in with Javier, your boyfriend. She told all the doctors that living with Javier would increase the chances that you would follow your medical protocol, that Javier could reach you better than she or the doctors or nurses ever could. But it was not your need for medicine alone that guided her. There was another force, a force that challenged her values as mother—for your brother and sister would never receive the same privileges that you did. This same force guided your mother through all the decisions she later made in caring for you: love, for you and for what you were about to lose.

This was her true motivation. And the decisions she made may have surprised and even rattled your physicians, but it was you she had in mind. Always.

And when the sad day came for her to tell your family how grave your medical condition had become, it was everyone's voice she wanted to hear, not just the voices of the doctors who told her there was nothing more they could do. She wanted to hear from your younger brother Daniel and your little sister Isabella; from your aunts and uncles; from your grandmother; and, of course, from Javier. Your mother wanted everyone to understand what was truly happening to you; she wanted all their questions to be answered. She requested that I be present at this meeting, because she knew she could not face your entire family alone. She was particularly worried about your brother Daniel, for she knew that he would be the least able to bear the news of your impending death. He would not allow the family to decide to let you die.

That morning I met with your family in the sunny living room of your mother's house. Your relatives did not speak English, so your mother translated into Spanish the words that would help them to understand what was happening to you. Specifically the doctors had told your mother that your body was not getting better, and that the cancer inside was stronger than the medicine they had left to give. They told her that continuing the treatments might only be more painful as well as unkind. Palliation, pain management, was their plan.

Daniel would not allow these words to reach his heart. "We will not stop," he pleaded. "Mama, don't let the doctors stop."

It was Javier who spoke up and gently tried to calm your brother. He understood what your mother was saying. He ran over to Daniel and held him, trying to make Daniel see what he saw, and knew, and had accepted as your fate.

You were transferred from the pediatric intensive care unit to a private room on the adolescent floor. I sat there with your mother night after night as she told me stories of her youth, of her life in South America with your father; of how she had fled his abusive hands and found her way to the United States. She talked of how she struggled in this country to earn enough money to bring you and your younger brother and sister to the new home she had created. She described how she managed to buy one airplane ticket, and how she convinced your father to allow you, her oldest child, to come to America for a chance at a better future. She smiled as she remembered the sweet but difficult days when the two of you, mother and daughter, were "alone in America." One by one she was able to get all three of her children together again. Finally, after years of hardship, she cared for all three of you under one roof again.

Your mother was a wonderful storyteller. She remembered every detail of your childhood. She spoke of you quietly and with love in her voice. She saw things in you that you yourself had not believed were possible. And she had a vision of your life from the very day you were born: she wanted you to have an American education; she wanted you to find your own special talent; she wanted you to have friends.

I remember how she sat quietly by your side at the hospital one day as your best friend painted your fingernails. You were too weak to see how pretty they were, but your friend painted them anyway. She stroked your hands and carefully massaged your fingers with your favorite vanilla oil. As she did, your mother smiled and watched as you two girls acted out a common scene in an uncommon place. She was quiet in her pain. No one knew how hard your mother struggled to make all your dreams come true, even as the world around her crumbled.

It was no surprise to me when I learned that, suddenly, Javier had asked you to marry him, that there was to be a wedding that very evening, and that your mother would arrange the whole affair. The wedding would be held at your bedside—you were too weak to be moved and could not stay awake for long. Your mother explained that Javier had asked for your hand in marriage that very morning. She told me that, when you told her the news, she gently asked you when you planned to marry.

"When I get better," you replied.

But your mother knew that time was not on your side. She feared that if you waited too long, either you or Javier might change your minds. So, without further ado, she left your bedside for three hours to plan a wedding—your wedding.

"It has to be perfect," she was overheard saying. "Today is my daughter's wedding day." When she returned, you would become a bride.

When I arrived that evening, your room was already filling with relatives. The doctors, nurses, and Child Life specialists had all heard the good news and were gathering to honor you on your big day. Your aunts were dressed in evening gowns; their hair was done up and their makeup freshly applied. During the ceremony a tape recorder in the corner would play "Here Comes the Bride" while your brother Daniel stood by the window and videotaped the whole event. Your sister would be your maid of honor, and your little cousin would be the flower girl. Not a detail was missed, not even the rice.

This part of the story you may not know, but I believe it is important to tell it to you. Shortly after I had arrived, I was called into the office of the hospital administrator. I was told that because you were still a minor, and your boyfriend already eighteen years of age, your wedding could not legally be allowed to take place. The doctors were impressed that your mother had handled most of the details of this wedding, but in her haste to make your last wish come true, she had not considered the laws of the state or the rules of the hospital.

What your mother had not planned, however, fate planned. You see, the priest from your mother's parish was unable to preside over your wedding on such short notice, and the priest who would be able to officiate did not, I learned, have a license to marry couples in the state of New York. So for better or worse, because it was not going to be a legal marriage, all obstacles with regard to the rules of the hospital were lifted. Your mother begged me not to tell you, for this was her last gift to you. You would be married that night, and it did not matter to her whether your marriage was legal in the eyes of the state: it would be a marriage in the eyes of God. And so, by some divine accident or an act of fate, your wedding was under way.

Cover your eyes. Her mother is coming with the wedding gown. It is bad luck to see the bride in her gown before the ceremony. Cover the windows. Close the curtain and keep the guests out. It is not yet time.

Where is the groom?

He is on his way.

Your mother and her sister brought your beautiful wedding dress to your bed. Was it satin or silk? It was covered with lace and mother-of-pearl and embroidered throughout with countless little butterflies. The doctors told your mother that you were too weak to be moved. It would not be possible to stand you up to dress you. So, with trembling hands and loving eyes, your mother gently placed your pale, thin arms through the sleeves of that dress. Your chest and stomach, filled with cancer, were covered by the pearl-encrusted bodice of your beautiful gown as it lay carefully over you like a warm blanket. The butterflies on your gown shone elegantly in the reflected light of a nearby window.

Your makeup, that was to be next. It had to be perfect. Your head, hairless from chemotherapy, was covered by a beautiful hat. Your face would be made to glow with irrepressible hope and touches of rouge and eye shadow. This was your special day, and you would become a princess.

Where is the groom?
Somebody saw him in the corner.
Why isn't he getting dressed?
Last minute jitters? Oh, the youth today.

I found your groom sitting quietly on the other side of your hospital curtain, not quite ready to put on his tuxedo.

"May I speak with you?" he asked.

"Yes, Javier. What is it?"

"I don't think I can go through with this," he said. "I don't . . . I didn't think this would all happen so fast. Not today . . . not like this."

He began to explain that because of his love for you, he had wanted to make you smile, to make you laugh one more time before you died. He explained that he wanted to marry you; truly he did. But he did not realize that after his proposal your mother would arrange such a beautiful and complete wedding so quickly. He told me that he was happy you had said yes, but he thought that, if you got better, the two of you would plan your wedding day together. And if you were not to make it home from this hospital stay . . . well, he had not, could not, think that far.

Cover her feet. The ballet slippers, white with pale satin bows, they must fit. All brides wear pretty white shoes. Raise her bed so that she can look at herself in the mirror. She is so pretty.

Javier and I sat there for a long while. Quietly he told me that he was afraid of all that a marriage commitment entailed.

"I am so young. I'm only eighteen," he explained.

"Do you want to change your mind, Javier?"

"No, no," he answered. "I cannot do such a thing to Paloma. Not now. Not ever."

"What are you most afraid of, right at this very moment?"

"I don't know," he cried. "I guess I'm just not ready to think of myself as married. But I love her. I do. And I want her to smile. I want her to smile."

"What if I were to tell you that this wedding may not be a legal union in the eyes of the state? What if, for some strange reason, your marriage contract were not signed by a licensed, practicing priest?"

"What are you saying to me?" he asked.

"What I am saying is this: can you stand here before Paloma and before your friends and family and express your commitment of love to her, knowing that, whether the law recognizes this as legitimate or not, it will be a marriage in the eyes of love and of God?"

For a moment he was silent, and I knew that he understood what I was asking. Slowly, with gathering courage and conviction, he said, "Yes. Yes I do. I will do this. This is right. It will be a marriage before God."

Hurry, hurry. The room is filling up with guests. Where is the priest? Is he ready? The music! Now is the time for music.

Get the camera ready. Now is the time.

"I have no best man," Javier exclaimed. "Will you be my best man?"

"I would be honored, Javier," I said. "I would be truly honored."

"And my shoes. I forgot my tuxedo shoes."

"Who wears a size nine-and-a-half around here?" I asked.

"I do," the priest answered as he readied his prayer book for the event.

"Let me have them," I said. "The groom can't get married without shoes."

And there, by the refracted light of the fluorescent bulbs overhead, in a place somehow larger than life, a barefoot priest, your frightened groom, and you, a frail but radiant bride, began your wedding ceremony.

Between one moment and the next, we age twenty years. Or so it seems. Javier stood there at your side, sure of himself and of his love for you, and ready to be your husband.

"Place the ring on your bride's finger," the priest instructed.

With trembling hands and gentle eyes, Javier carefully raised your finger to meet the ring that would be yours until death. Then, with grace and loving-kindness, he gathered your fingers around his so that with his careful guidance you could place a ring on his wedding finger as well.

The music played quietly in that small hospital room, and everyone stood breathless as you and your groom once again defied expectations and lived life the way you dreamed it should be. The priest asked if "anyone gathered here today had any reason why these two should not be joined together in marriage."

"Speak now or forever hold your peace," he said.

And there was silence.

"Then in the eyes of all who are here today, and in the eyes of God, I hereby pronounce you man and wife. You may kiss the bride."

We stood breathless—doctors, nurses, relatives, and friends. We cried as Javier bent down to kiss you. We celebrated with laughter and joy as you married your love on that fateful, bittersweet night. Your brother recorded it all on videotape. For months after that day your mother would carry that tape with her wherever she went. She would show it to everyone who wanted to see the video of her daughter's wedding.

The nurses took Polaroid snapshots of every moment that passed and, in no time at all, they presented you with your very own wedding album. It was complete with pictures of you with your mother, your new mother-in-law, and of course your new groom. The wedding cake, store-bought and in a box, was sweeter than any made by the finest chefs of New York. And the flowers, which were ordinarily forbidden in a room for an immune-suppressed patient, were portioned out to each of your guests as wedding favors.

Cover the windows. Close the curtains. Her eyes are too sensitive to the light.

In the dark, when their wedding is over, he will sit quietly by her side. Sitting in silence, he will stare into her gaze, which now stretches across time and galaxies. "What do you see?" he will ask her silently. "Where are you going?"

He will not leave her side for a moment, not even after the nurses suggest that he go into the waiting room for a well-deserved nap. He will lie beside her in that hospital bed and dream of a life with her that will never be. He will not go home to change his clothes or to shower. He will tell them that this is his wedding night and that he will not leave her.

In only twenty-four hours her mother will fall to the floor. "Why are they taking the oxygen away?" she will scream. "No. She needs more air. Call the doctor. Tell him to give her some more medicine. Tell him she needs more chemotherapy."

She is confused. She will say that she knows her daughter is dead. That she has to take care of her other little ones. That she has to be strong for them. But she remains there, unable to move, unable to say goodbye.

Her brother will stand motionless in the corner, unbelieving of all that is happening.

"Wake up, wake up! Tell her to wake up," he will cry. He will throw himself on her, weeping, stroking her head, her eyes, her cheeks, her mouth. But her breathless body will not move.

Her mother will tell him that it is time to go, but he will not listen. "Open her eyes," he will cry. "Somebody open her eyes."

Her mother will say to him, "She is no more. She is now in your heart. She will not open her eyes anymore."

And with all the energy she has as a mother, she will ask him to help her to the hospital door and into the car to take her home.

When you died, I stood in awe of your passing spirit. I do not remember much about what happened next, but when I looked up, Javier stood before me.

"I know I should be sad, and I am sad, but I am really not inside," he told me. "I made her so happy, and it makes me happy now to know that she was happy. My wife. She is my wife for eternity."

He told me that he had whispered to you that it was time to go to Jesus, time to meet his little brother and sister who are in heaven and who will take good care of you there.

"I know this is better," he said. "When we were dating she said 'Love me forever.' And I will. I will love for eternity. I saw she was breathing," he went on. "Everyone said that she had stopped breathing. But I saw her chest moving very slowly. And I leaned over and kissed her on the lips. And I went 'Whoa!' because her lips were so cold. And then . . . she stopped breathing."

"You ushered her into the next world with a kiss," I said.

"Yeah, I guess I did. And I am happy that you know this, because I made her smile and she was happy. I did a good thing and I have no regrets. I'm glad I married her."

Six years have passed since your wedding day. I visited your mother several times that first year after you died. We sat in your living room and talked of your wedding and of your life and what might have been.

And yes, I called Javier on your first wedding anniversary. He was living with your mother and younger brother and sister, and had gone back to college. He told me that no one else had called on that anniversary day, but that it did not matter because he was remembering you then and would remember you forever as his bride.

I lost touch with your family after that. I was told that your mother had taken your family down South to begin a new life. And Javier, your husband, I don't know where he went after they moved. But I know in my heart that, wherever he is, you are by his side.

⌒ POSTSCRIPT

What can be said about the place of love in the healing process? We know that we are mortal and separate beings; we are born alone and we must die alone. But the lessons that love has to teach us are infinite and everlasting. They can carry us through days of sublime togetherness as well as nights of loneliness and despair. We know that as human beings we have transcended nature; that we have been pulled from the harmony of man and earth, fetus and mother; and we are meant to journey forward as separate individuals. We have a capacity for reason, and through our reason we discover that our deepest fear is also our greatest need: to overcome our aloneness; to be free of the prison of solitude. For without a sense of union with another—a soul mate, a loving partner—we feel uncertain, anxious, helpless, and even ashamed.

So we search for love. Erich Fromm says that of all forms of learning, love is the only one that profits the soul. We seek love as the mature answer to the question of our existence. A union with another preserves our uniqueness and assures us that we matter, that we will be remembered long after we are gone. This connection is an achievement that can only be experienced inwardly. And when we have attained it we feel alive, even in the face of our own mortality. For when we love, whether or not we receive love in return, we express our commitment to this life.

Love, like grief, requires labor, respect, and nurturing. In our search for connection and relief from solitude, we find that we must sometimes wrestle with our greatest fears; we turn inward to the pain we feel, and await a blessing of relief. Love also asks us to be aware of ourselves and others—to look honestly and even admiringly at the goals and challenges that fate has set before us. As we watch and observe ourselves and those around us, we gain a greater ability to grow into independent beings, free from the fears that once held us in place. Last, like grief, love asks for nurturance, for the care and attention that gently help it to grow, change, and transform us as it unfolds.

We stand before love as pupils. One lesson that love teaches, says Rilke, is that what has died from us has died *into* us, into our hearts and our memories. What was once visible to the eye and to the world is now only deeply embedded within. The spirit, the essence of our beloved continues to influence, sustain, and support us. As we grow, the relationship with our loved one deepens. In surviving grief, we honor and glorify love. In time we take on new challenges, we speak with a stronger voice, and we do things that our loved one would have wanted to do if he or she were still alive. We perform the deeds and rituals that our beloved can no longer perform. We create memorials and monuments, living representations of a life that once was, and we share our love with everyone who wants to hear. In the process we discover that though love in the physical sense is gone from us, it is only a hand's breadth away in the things we touch, both inside and out. It is in the decisions we make and in the words we speak. We discover that love continues endlessly as long as we honor its presence in our lives. In so doing, we come to realize that we have achieved the essential task of man's existence: we are separate, but with love in our hearts, we are forever connected.

In the end, perhaps the greatest lesson of love is that there really is no death, only grief. Love and the energy that love creates live on, even through the transformation from the physical to the spiritual. As long as there is love, we know we can survive our grief until we meet again in a place, or dimension, where love is all there is.

3

A Lesson in Strength

To be afraid is to be brave.
—anonymous (age six)

Dear Matthew,

"A special child." That's what you might have been called by those who never truly knew you. "One of God's children." "Different." But these adjectives deny your true character, for words can never describe your essence. You were not "slow," though your classmates may have called you this because you could not keep up with them socially. You were not "challenged," though this is what your teachers may have said about your academic abilities. True, your speech was measured and often difficult to understand, but the expressions you used were gilded with the colors and images of poetry. Yes, your gait was unsteady, mostly the result of the brain surgery you had, but the path you wished to follow was straight and clear: "teacher for children with disabilities," you told me. "This is what I want to be when I grow up."

Delicate. Gifted. Cautious. Aware. These adjectives suit you better, for you were keenly aware of all that happened around and inside of you. I remember how on the day we met, you asked me what adults meant by the term "growth." This was your mother's word for the tumor that had just been removed from your brain. She did not want you to know that you had cancer, that you were regularly visiting an oncology clinic so that the doctors could carefully measure the precarious success of your surgery. You would not need chemotherapy, but radiation would be a part of your treatment.

"What is radiation?" you asked.

"It's like a thin ray of light that focuses directly on the place where the growth was," I explained to you. "Like sunshine on a pimple, it makes it get smaller and smaller until it's gone forever." The idea of radiation was foreign to you and, because it would be focused on the back of your head, you would not be able to see what was happening.

"Okay, Norman. I understand," you said. But your broken smile and your silent stare belied your straightforward response.

With one hand tied behind my back, I tried to guide you through the land of recovery, relapse, and grief. But I realize now that on some level, you always knew what your mother never wanted to reveal: that while your brain tumor was gone, it would inevitably return and take with it all the mystery and beauty that defined you.

You were the older of two children in a family that was silently dissolving from the trauma that cancer brought into your home. Your father did not always speak to your mother about you, and they did not always agree on your upbringing. Your mother told me that nights would pass without your father's return home, how his work seemed to keep him away more than usual. Still, after a medical treatment or a major surgery, both of them were there, holding your hands and caressing your face.

Your mother wanted me to speak with you after your first brain surgery. She feared that you might have worries about the recovery process ahead. You were sullen and unsure of me at first, but as we began to talk, you opened your heart. You talked of your surgery and of your fears, of your family and your dreams. You spoke of the weekend ahead, of the snow that fell outside my office window, and of your love of the holiday season.

"It's Christmas. Would you like to take one of these toys home with you?" I asked.

"That's okay. Thank you anyway," you declined. But there, in the corner of the room, was a soft, furry lion you shyly wished to hold.

"Take it," I said. "It stands for courage and strength. Your courage, Matthew, your strength."

And you smiled, and asked, "Really?"

"Yes, really. Take him home. He's yours."

There, on Christmas Eve, with a lion, a lie, and a wish for a happier ending, our story began.

Your mother and I agreed that we would meet in my private office every Wednesday morning. I feared that the oncology clinic was too noisy a place to allow us to sit and play together peacefully. Besides, seeing the doctors and nurses there might make you wonder more about your condition. These were my thoughts as I opened the door to the waiting room every Wednesday. There, in the corner of that small anteroom, you waited patiently for the chance to play another game of cards and to talk with your new friend about life. Week after week I watched as you carefully got up from your chair and walked slowly into my office. Once inside, we sat together on the floor and talked about the days since our last visit together.

"How are you today, Dr. Norman? Did you have a good week?"

This is how we spent that cold winter. We played cards, told stories, and compared notes on another week of life. You taught me how to play your favorite action-hero card game. You quizzed me on the names of each character, on their strengths, weaknesses, and special powers. You even bought me my own pack of cards so that I could practice between sessions. You were my teacher and I was your protégé. I never quite understood that card game, and my inability to catch on seemed to provide you with a guilty sense of delight. I usually lost at these games. You always smiled.

"That's okay, Dr. Norman. It's okay to lose sometimes."

"Yes, I know, Matthew. It's okay."

One afternoon, when we were not involved in our usual card tournament, you turned to me with tears in your eyes. From within a strange and heavy silence, your question finally arose.

"Can you keep a secret?" you asked.

"Yes," I assured you.

"Will you tell my mother?"

"Not if you don't want me to."

"I need to tell you something. It's very important."

With tears filling your eyes, you tried to tell me that you knew. You knew that the "growth" in your head was a tumor. You knew that it was cancer. You knew that it was coming back. You knew that your mother and father and I were not being totally honest with you.

"Say it, Matthew," I said to myself. "Say that you know." But you never spoke. You just sat and cried. And when your mother came in to take you home, she saw that you were crying. She leaned toward you and touched your face and smiled.

"It's okay, Matthew," she said. "You can tell me what's wrong."

But you knew that you could not. You knew that you could not hurt her with your awareness of the truth. She did not want you to know that you had relapsed and that you were sicker than you appeared. Ever obedient, you sat smiling and loving her. You said nothing.

I met with your mother after that day, and I suggested that it was time you were told the truth about the "growth" in your head—that it was indeed a tumor, that it had a name, that the name was cancer, and that the cancer had returned. But she declined to follow my lead. She did not think it would be helpful for you to know, and I did not argue. Your mother knew you better than anyone else. She was your guardian angel, and I knew that she had your best interests at heart.

As time wore on, your visits to my office became less frequent as you became less able to leave your house. On those rare occasions when you felt strong enough, your mother brought you to my office in your wheelchair for a short visit. Sometimes we set up my desk in such a way that you could play cards from your wheelchair. Other times I sat on the floor by your side and told you stories of the week that had just passed. The medicine you took for your pain made you tired, and you often drifted in and out of sleep. Even so, when I asked you if wanted to take a rest or go home, you opened your eyes and said, "No. Not yet."

I thought you deserved to experience for yourself the pride we all felt as you courageously fought your battle with cancer. I felt you needed to hold on to something, like the gentle stuffed lion whose soft fur you touched whenever you were afraid.

"Do you know what a foot soldier is, Matthew?" I asked.

"A foot soldier?" You always answered my questions with a question. "Why yes, Dr. Norman. I think he is the first man on the ground to fight in a war."

"Yes, Matthew. That's right. And in my opinion, a foot soldier is the bravest soldier in the war." Then I added, "And you, my friend, are a true foot soldier."

"Me?" you responded. "But what war am I fighting?"

"The growth, Matthew. The growth in your head. You battle this every day, don't you?"

"Well, yes, I do. It is like a war. A war against growth terrorism," you replied.

And there, on that cold day in December, you enlisted as a foot soldier in the war against cancer. I told you about an organization I had created, modeled on David Epston's work on narrative therapy for critically ill children. I called it the Long Island Association of Foot Soldiers. It was a club whose members included children of different ages with varying medical obstacles to overcome. Like you, some had been in the hospital for many weeks; others were struggling with the loss of hair or other difficult side effects of treatment. I told you that all you had to do to become a member was to write a letter to the president of the organization explaining, in your own words, why you should be accepted.

With pencil in hand, you began to write:

Dear Ms. President,

I think that I should be a Foot Soldier because I've been much worse than I normaly expexted. I kept on having grouths all over my head and I see the good docs every Wensday. Then much later I had something that really hurt me a lot. I had an infection right after the trip to Disney World.

I have been in the hospital for at least I don't know a cuple of months. All the time I was thinking those important words: Get well and get out of bed and I did this but I am still at home getting a lot of easy treatment from Dr. Weiss. And I have made more wonderful friends here and I am having a good time.

I hope you agree with me this is why I should be a Foot Soldier. I hope you understand this is why I should be one. I'll be looking forward to hear and see you soon. Signed

One of your very good friends,

Matthew

You wrote with a hand weakened from battle. When you felt too tired to continue, you dictated the rest to me. You had a feverish desire to say as much as you could in your letter, and you were eager to mail it that very same day. Together we addressed the envelope, stamped it, and wheeled down to the corner where, letter in hand, you proudly put it in the mailbox.

That would be your last visit to my office. The pain you experienced was growing stronger, and you would be transferred to a hospital for chronically and terminally ill children. The day of your transfer, I met you in the oncology clinic. You were resting in the dark in a big pink easy chair. Your mother and her best friend were by your side. The IV pole behind your chair supplied you with a transfusion of platelets for clotting and pain medicine for comfort.

I entered your treatment room and asked if I could read a letter to you. It was the reply from the Long Island Association of

Foot Soldiers, and I knew it would make you smile. Surrounded by all your doctors and nurses, social workers and secretaries, I read the president's reply aloud:

> Dear Matthew,
>
> Thank you for your letter. I, too, think that you deserve to be a member of our association. Any boy who has had to face so much medical treatment and still smiles and knows how to have fun is definitely qualified to be a Foot Soldier!!
>
> How are your spirits? You sounded very positive in your letter/application. Tell me, how do you keep your attitude up? That is the very thing that can help you through your difficult days.
>
> I welcome you wholeheartedly into our Corps. You are hereby awarded status and title of "#1 Foot Soldier in the War Against Growth Terrorism," on this, the 12th of December in the year two thousand and one; complete with all of the rights, privileges and honors appertaining thereto.
>
> Congratulations, young man, and welcome. I look forward to hearing more about you in the months and years ahead.
>
> Yours very truly,
The President of the Long Island
Association of Foot Soldiers

With tears in your eyes, you held that letter close and smiled the smile of a hero. And because a letter alone did not seem to be enough of a symbol of your strength and courage, your mother and I had another surprise for you. You beamed with delight as we presented you with a silver trophy as you had once told your mother you wanted to receive one day. Engraved on the base were these words:

MATTHEW P. #1 FOOT SOLDIER
IN THE WAR AGAINST GROWTH TERRORISM

I was told that you carried that trophy with you wherever you went. I was told that you slept with it alongside your furry lion each night. I was informed by your mother that these were with you when you left this world a few weeks later. And we at the hospital—your troop of soldiers, doctors, nurses, social workers, and friends—all stood in silence when we learned of your passing.

Now we are left here without you. And here, on this side of heaven, we continue as foot soldiers in the battle against growth terrorism, against cancer, and against the pain of living.

I pray that you are at peace and I pray that you are in no pain. I pray that one day we will all meet again, in a place where there is no need for strife, anger, or even strength. Only love.

↶ POSTSCRIPT

What is the lesson that death tries to teach us about strength and courage? And how are we to survive the pain of dying when the very act of living indisposes us to loss? The paradox of living is that we know we must eventually die. Even so, throughout our lives we search for protection from our mortality; we spend our days with "both feet on the earth," cloaked in denial and fear. We are busily involved in the mundane and accountable to many social relationships. But then death enters our lives and we find ourselves relating less with the world. We become disconnected from the ordinary routines of daily life, and we find that we live "with one foot in heaven." We feel accountable to no one, or perhaps only to our lost loved one—to a spirit, a memory, an essence. We spend our days ruminating in pain; we discover that we envy those who are blessed with ignorance, for they are able to ignore the signs of death and disrepair. We who are cursed with insight, however, focus solely on the vision of what we once knew and loved. Some of us cease to live; we avoid rooms in our own homes, we stop going to restaurants we used to frequent and to places where we once traveled together. Our memories now haunt us, and our life diminishes as we run from the pain that we fear awaits us at every corner.

How, then, do we develop the strength to tolerate our fear, to survive the pain of living? And how can we eventually grow from it? As mourners, we must first redefine what is meant by the word "strength": that in crying we are not weak, fragile, or guilty of "giving in" to sadness. "Being strong" may actually mean having the wisdom to know when to be weak. It is through crying that we gain mastery over our loss. When we honor our private pain we recognize that it is the weak among us who have the courage to feel. We discover that in "falling down" we muster the strength to rise again. And as we rise, we find ourselves on a circular, not a linear path—"getting better" means that we are better able to endure the pain we feel. We come to understand that tears, like rain, must be plentiful. This is the path we must all travel; it is this difficult experience that distinguishes us from mere survivors and makes us contributing, thriving citizens of the world.

We discover that grief is like a muscle. A good cry, a good "workout," leaves us feeling sore and aching. But with time, and with the repetition of the sorrow it bears, our grief muscle strengthens. We do not run from our brokenness. We struggle with it and befriend it, allowing the tears to flow. And when we are finished, we begin again, for our "workout" has no time frame or calendar. Our goal is that one day we will carry our burden, our sorrow, with greater ease. We only hope that those around us respect and honor us in our moments of weakness.

As we grow through our pain, we discover other ways of gaining strength. Strength for many of us comes through caring for surviving family members.

As one mother told me:

> I have another child who needs me who I have totally neglected. He has spent weeks with my in-laws and he misses me so much. And I realize that it's time for me to take a little care of my family. So I went around the house and I cleaned up all this stuff. For six months I let this house go. I let myself go. But you have to understand that I didn't do this to get rid of Jimmy, or to push his memory away. I did it because I can't let my other child get caught up in the mess that I am in. Jimmy is in heaven now and he wouldn't want all of us crying all day, every day.

For others, strength comes from religion or from spiritual beliefs, teachings, and practices. The relationship we have with a personal God or with a religious community helps us construct meaning in our struggle and may make us more resilient. As one mourner wrote to me:

> I miss her terribly. But I know she is where she has to be. I think differently than most nonbelievers. I know that things are different in heaven, and I know that our time on earth is only like the blink of an eye. And I am comforted by the knowledge that, by the time I get up there, my daughter won't even have missed me. That's what our lifetime is to them up in heaven.

We discover, additionally, that strength comes from knowing who we are. We must continue to ask ourselves important questions about our own identities: What do I believe in? What are the values, likes, and dislikes that make me special and unique? Unfortunately, those who have suffered a loss struggle with changes in identity and role. We are no longer someone's brother, mother, or father. As one mourner put it:

> I see his lacrosse equipment in every room, and I hear him rolling around on my hardwood floors with his skates. He is all over the house, but really, he is nowhere. Now the house is quiet. I miss the busy dynamics of my old life, when I had to run to work, then come home and run to soccer practice, then dance rehearsal, make dinner and then help with the homework, and yell at him to stop making so much noise. Now it's all so quiet. If I'm not his mother, then who am I?

We have been changed by the course of life's events, and we have lost our place in the world. Through our sorrow we have also lost, as the trauma specialist Beverly James suggests, the luxury of knowing an "authentic self." We may feel numb from our pain, or we may hide or disown our negative feelings for fear that people will not understand. Our recovery involves the reawakening of our senses: we must remember the smell of flowers and the feel of the sun on the back of our neck. In addition, we must allow ourselves to become immersed in our memories. In reconnecting with our earlier, happier selves, we remind ourselves of who we once were and of who we are capable of becoming once again.

Most important, we learn that broken hearts, unlike broken bicycles or shattered vases, cannot be mended. We know that our hearts will never be whole again, and we are not afraid to accept the fact that we are changed. We are not looking for quick fixes or kind words of repair. Broken and bereaved, we are soothed by the presence of people who let us feel our sorrow, no matter the discomfort it causes.

Eventually we discover that by exploring our darkest emotions and by embracing the pain that awaits us in grief, we learn new ways of living. We create new connections—we go to new restaurants and visit places we've never seen before. We find that we are excited about the prospect of a new coat or angered by the ordinary bustle of traffic jams and missed appointments. We dare to live with both feet on the earth again, and, as one patient put it, with "only one hand raised toward heaven." We surround ourselves with people who, like us, have had the courage to wrestle with their sorrows and have survived and been blessed. They, like us, are aware that it is through enduring the struggles of life that we redefine ourselves. We are bereft, and we are weak, but we now know what it means to be truly brave and strong.

4

A Lesson in Understanding

That which has been created with love [cannot] be abandoned.
—Madeleine L'Engle

Dear Rachel,

"Heaven is like a two-family house, where God lives upstairs and Grandma lives downstairs," said one child. "It's a beautiful place with lots of toys, and everyone wears long white T-shirts that match their wings," said another. Children's views of the afterlife are often marked by personal wishes for magic and restored health; by the belief that a change from the physical to a spiritual realm is accomplished through a loving act of God; or that long-forgotten ancestors have prepared a newer, safer place for them where they may grow and heal. But your story, and the story of where you went after you died, is empty of the magic that carries so many mourners through the treacherous land of grief. Your family never believed in a heaven, angels, or an afterlife.

What soothed or comforted your survivors? Where did you go, Rachel? And if there is no heaven, then how do we think about you? These questions haunted me as I sat with your family, especially your big brother, who was only four years old at the time of your death. What was the message in your painful transformation from life to death? You were so young—too small even to know your own name, too weak to say "Mama." After only a few short months of life, your life was over.

You were not unloved. You were cherished and coddled by your sweet mother. You were held lovingly by your father as he softly swayed and sang you songs from his own childhood. And your brother, at four, read words to you that he had only just begun to decipher from the many books given to you when you were born. You smiled a lot, and your eyes reflected the safety and warmth that your mother and father gave you.

"What do we tell her brother? How do we explain this to him?" your parents asked me.

"You tell him that the hurt in her head is not getting better. You tell him that the medicine the doctors are giving her is not strong enough to make it go away."

"What if he fears that this will happen to him someday? How will we ever be able to assure him that most hurts can be cured?"

"You tell him that Rachel's illness is very rare, that this is a type of hurt that he will not get," I answered. "Tell him that it is not contagious, and that he can kiss her and hold her hand," I added. "And remind him how important he is to you and to the whole family."

The day the doctors told your mother that you were dying, she ran to a telephone and called your father to come quickly. "And bring Aaron," she insisted. "We are a family."

Your father walked into your hospital room with shock and surrender in his eyes. The battle was ending. Together your parents stood there, weakened and worn by unanswered prayers.

Your mother wanted to share these last precious moments with you quietly, lovingly, and as a family.

"Aaron, read your sister a story," she begged. Her voice was filled with sorrow as she watched you lie there with your frail little body dwarfed by the large pillows that surrounded you. "Aaron, read to her. You are so good at reading."

Your brother climbed up on your hospital bed, curled himself up in the corner near your little feet. Slowly, and without understanding why reading was so important at this moment, he opened his favorite, *Goodnight Moon*, to the first page and began to read to you.

In the great green room there was a telephone and a red balloon, and a picture of the cow jumping over the moon.

Your mother sat on one side of you, your father on the other, and each kissed you and whispered in your ear as your brother continued to read aloud.

And there were three little bears sitting on chairs, and two little kittens, and a pair of mittens, and a little toy house, and a young mouse.

You stirred silently, your little hand still taped to the tiny wooden board used to administer intravenous medication and pain relief. Your father, broken from the long journey that had brought you to this point, gently stroked your bald head.

And a comb and a brush and a bowl full of mush and a quiet old lady whispering "hush."

Your mother wanted your brother to read to you so that he would not run around your room in frustration or boredom. For these moments with you would not come again. The hours of caressing you and singing you to sleep would soon end.

Goodnight room, goodnight moon, goodnight cow jumping over the moon. Goodnight light and the red balloon.

What was your mother thinking about in those sorrow-filled moments? Was she recalling the day you were born? And your father, was he praying for a miracle or even for one more hour?

Goodnight comb and goodnight brush. Goodnight nobody and goodnight mush. And goodnight to the old lady whispering "hush."

Lovingly your brother read, and his little voice filled that solemn room with light. He read the simple words of a children's book to you while, unbeknownst to him, you took your last breath.

Goodnight stars, goodnight air, goodnight noises everywhere.

I brought your brother into my office across the hall to play so that your mother and father could be alone with you. He did not know what had happened in that dark room across the hall, only that he had read a favorite story to you and had made you feel better.

I visited your family two days later. Your house was filled with guests wishing your mother and father the speedy healing that those unafflicted by grief mistakenly believe is possible. I found your brother out in the backyard looking up at the sky.

"What are you doing, Aaron?" I asked.

"I'm looking for a bird."

"A bird? What for?"

"To bring a message to the moon, where my sister is," he replied.

"And what would you tell her?"

"I want to tell her to come home. Come home soon, Rachel."

My friendship with your mother and father, and with Aaron, grew deeper and stronger after those sad days. I spent many hours with your brother, trying to help him obey your parents—get to bed on time and keep his room clean. But he was preoccupied with two questions that no one could sufficiently answer for him.

"Where is my sister?" he would ask me. "And when is she coming home?"

I struggled with an answer for him, for I knew that your parents did not believe in a heaven or in a life after death. And indeed, they felt sorely unprepared to explain to Aaron what had happened to you and where you had gone.

"She is in your heart," your mother would tell him. But at age four, your brother did not understand how someone your size could fit inside his heart, or how you might have gotten there.

"Tell him that his sister's body stopped working," I offered. "Tell him that she no longer breathes, or burps, or laughs. Then explain to him that her body was placed in a box and that the box was put into the ground."

"I cannot tell him these things," your mother cried.

"Why not?" I asked.

"Don't you think he is too young to know about graves?" she asked. "And what about when it rains? And all of the insects?"

"I'm afraid I don't understand."

"If it rains," your mother explained, "won't he worry that she is getting wet? Won't he be scared about all the bugs underground?"

I waited in silence for some way to answer your parents' questions. I could not sanitize death. I could not assure them that any or all of these things were not true. Instead I struggled to separate the feelings and fears that belonged specifically to your parents from those that belonged to Aaron. I tried to help them understand that without an answer to his question, your brother's imagination might run wild and cause him undue pain and confusion.

Your mother cried as she struggled to make sense of my words. Your parents sat quietly and slowly recognized that their own journey through the dark land of grief would be a different one from that of their son.

One week later, your brother came to me with a smile. With pride in his voice, he leaned over and pulled me in close.

"I have a secret," he whispered.

"You do? And what is your secret?" I asked him.

"I know where my sister is."

"You do? Where is your sister?"

"She's in the sanitary."

"The sanitary? What's a sanitary?"

"It's a place where people go when they die. They put their bodies in a box and they put the box in the ground. And it's nice there. They have trees and big stones. And I can go there anytime I want, and if I want to visit my sister all I have to do is sit by her stone and I can talk to her or read her a story."

We smiled together because Aaron had finally learned where he could find you. He never asked about what happens when it rains, or about cold weather or bugs. I never spoke of heaven, nor of the soul, nor of a life beyond. These were things that your family was unsure of, and I wanted to respect their wishes.

I am happy that Aaron found you. I know that he visits you and talks about you a lot. You have two new brothers now, born several years after you died. When people ask Aaron about his family, he says, "I have two brothers and one sister." And when they ask how old you are and where you are he says, "Rachel is always in my heart. She died when I was very young, but I visit her often, because I know where she is."

And when he looks up at the sky and sees the moon rising, he smiles because he has a secret that he now can share: he knows where you are, and that you are safe and well.

⌒ POSTSCRIPT

What can children teach us about death? And how can their appreciation of life and loss, though different from what adults know and believe, guide us toward healthier ways of coping? In helping children come to terms with loss, there is much that we ourselves can learn about our own fears, wishes, and beliefs. In understanding the views that children have of death and loss more clearly, we may learn new lessons about grief and recovery.

Magical thoughts are prominent features of all children's cognitive processes. So when talking about death to children, we discover that they understand and speak a different language than adults, especially during times of change and stress. Their vocabulary about loss is filled with metaphor, magic, and sometimes peril. Fantasies of angels, ghosts, and mythical characters often pervade the internal world of the grieving child.

Moreover, depending upon the child's age, death and all that accompanies it take on new and changing definitions. Thus, in sharing our feelings of grief with our children, and in listening closely to theirs, we adults need to be aware of the developmental changes that our children's cognitions undergo.

In particular, researchers believe that, until their cognitive development reaches full maturity, children's perceptions of death are different from those of adults in three important ways. Before the age of seven or eight, children have not yet achieved an understanding that death is irreversible—that once a person dies, there is no returning to life; that death is universal—everyone dies, not just pets and old people; and that death is unavoidable—that whether caused by illness, accident, or injury, it is inevitable.

Children younger than age seven view death quite differently. We know, for instance, that before the age of three a child believes that only pets, not humans, die. Adults often find themselves performing the timeless rituals of burying a beloved hamster in the backyard or flushing a favorite fish down the toilet. These experiences provide the child with the healthy antecedents of a future appreciation of death, but at age three the deaths of pets are all that most children can cognitively understand. By the age of four, however, most children use the word "death" in their conversations. They are aware that the word brings sadness to the eyes of the adults around them, but "death" is not a word that is necessarily associated with sadness for them. This means that when our four-year-old asks us why we are crying, our explanation may not feel sufficient to him.

By age five children perceive of death as a condition of separation—in other words, dead people go to heaven. But for most five-year-old children there is still no real emotion attached to the reality of death. We will hear them ask questions such as, "I know that Grandpa is in heaven, but when is he coming home?" It is important to listen closely to these questions because embedded within them may be fantasies that a loved one went to heaven because of something the child did, or that "Daddy will see and finally come down from heaven to punish me" if I misbehave. It is only through asking our children about their own thoughts of death and an afterlife that we learn of their wishes, fears, and misconceptions. While some children may believe in a heaven filled with angels and lost loved ones, others may ruminate about magical processes that threaten to harm them.

When children reach the age of six, it is believed that they develop a concrete, or literal, understanding of death. We find ourselves explaining to our six-year-old that dead people "no longer burp, or hiccup, or cough." We assure them that a loved one who has died no longer feels pain and is not sad or lonely. We speak in a language that helps children understand that death involves the cessation of bodily functions as well as human emotions. At this age children begin to discover the causal connection between death and illness, old age, and accidents. In addition, six-year-old children come to understand that people of any age may die, not just the elderly or the sick.

At the ages of seven, eight, and nine, most children have developed a more mature understanding of what happens to a person when he dies. There is an increased interest in the rituals surrounding death. At these ages children are likely to express their sadness over a loss—sometimes through tears but more often through changes in behavior, appetite, and mood. Magical and literal thinking may persist, however; we may hear a child ask a question such as, "If Grandma was at the wake, why wasn't she awake?" Curiosity about death is more common at this age; we discover that we need to be more prepared to answer our children's questions with clear, simple, and truthful statements.

Regardless of the child's age and cognitive awareness, honest and open discussions with our children about death will yield valuable insights into our own experience of loss. In attempting to fully know what death means to our children, we inevitably learn more about our own fears, wishes, and beliefs. We may hear gory details from a child that we may be too afraid to acknowledge. We may ache silently from a child's frank wish for reunion or restoration. We learn that we do not have to be young and naive to dare to ask, "When will my loved one come home?" We begin to understand that there are many ways of expressing the need to remain attached to our lost loved one, and that no one need is more appropriate than the next.

The forbidden dreams and fears that children harbor about death, separation, and loss may be uncensored reflections of our own inner truths. We all are mourners afflicted by the pain that living has produced. But our children grieve too. And when we open our ears to the painful tales of their journey through loss and recovery, we come to understand that as parents we are human and do not have all the answers. In fact, we discover that there is an art to "not knowing"; that in being unsure and unaware, our children may tell us all that we need to know. Most important, we learn that in questioning the world as a child might, the things we do not know today may be revealed to us when we are older, wiser, and spiritually, if not cognitively, more able to understand them.

Until that day arrives, however, we commune with our children. We laugh with them, and we cry with them when they are ready. We allow our collective sorrow to comfort us as a family.

5

A Lesson in Belonging

Every blade of grass has its own angel, who bends over it and whispers,
"Grow, grow."

—*The Talmud*

D ear Eddie,
A mother's touch, a father's kiss, a hug, and an unspoken promise of belonging: I wonder, did you ever experience these things? Did you ever close your eyes at night with the smell of your mother's perfume on your neck, or hear your father's voice in your ear as your shoulder leaned into his?

You were so young—only four years old—to be initiated into the world of cancer, hair loss, and month-long hospital stays. It is said that joy brings us quickly into the hearts of others. But it was pain and a need to belong that drew you instantly into ours.

You were known as the Little Mayor of the Sixth Floor, the pediatric wing of the hospital that came to be your home. Where was your mother? Did she visit you late at night after we had all gone home? "She'll be here," you would say. "She'll be coming later." But we rarely saw her. Rather, it was the nurses who bought you new underwear to wear as you lay day after day in your hospital gown. And the treats that you asked for long after your bedtime—these too were the loving gifts of your medical family.

The doctors placed you in a large room with four beds, hoping it would feel more like a bunkhouse at summer camp than a pediatric oncology unit. You chose the bed in the corner nearest the door. I realize now that this was so that you could capture the attention of visitors who came to see other children. You would attract them with your smile and with your shiny bald head. All anyone had to do was to walk slowly by the door of your "bunkhouse" and they were pulled in. You knew you had them. Your ransom was a hug and a brief promise of return for more fun and games.

I remember how you and your roommate created a scheme to get candy from unsuspecting passersby. You and Christopher would stand sullenly in front of the food machines in the corner of the parents' lounge. Day after day the two of you could be found there, leaning against your IV poles with your monitors beeping loudly for effect. You would cast your sad eyes on hungry and worn-out visitors until eventually one of them gave in. Then we would find you running down the hall to your room, your IV poles gliding behind you and your arms filled with candy for your late-night snack.

One night, as I passed your room en route to the elevator, I saw you sitting alone in your bed. You were hooked up to the IV pole that supplied you with the lifesaving treatments you needed. I stepped in, said a quick hello, and once again was caught in the embrace of your sad eyes.

"Can I have a little soda, Norman?"

"No, Eddie. I'm afraid not. You know what the doctors said about too many liquids," I replied.

"Just a little soda?"

"I don't know, Eddie."

"How about we play a game then?"

Perhaps an hour later I found myself staring at my watch, tired from rigorous matches of balloon volleyball, Go Fish, and tic-tac-toe. Then, as I finally headed toward the door, you asked, "TV, Norman? Let's see what's on."

I remember how I sat with you on the floor of your hospital room as we watched cartoons on the television on the portable cart in the corner. I remember how you climbed into my lap and nestled your head on my chest before eventually falling asleep. I remember thinking at the time that all the medicine in the world wasn't as important as the one thing you truly needed: to belong to someone. You needed to be claimed, to be someone's little boy. And so I sat with you for another hour, holding you as you slept, thinking about how much mothers and fathers love their children, and about how your parents could not find their way to you. I prayed for your healing and for your safety.

When you died, I was called to your room to give the news to Christopher, your partner in crime. At six he was too little to understand that dying meant that you would never come back. I sat with him a long while and carefully explained that your body had stopped working. I told him how a body is like a cocoon, and that inside this cocoon is a beautiful butterfly waiting to come out and fly to heaven.

He asked me what heaven was like, and I told him that I did not know. I asked him what he thought about heaven, and he told me that he thought it was a beautiful place with big white fields and toys. "Lots and lots of toys," he said. "And all the toys have the Jesus label on them," he said. "They're Jesus' toys, and Eddie can play with them any time he wants."

He told me that you will visit your mother every night when she is sleeping, that you will kiss her face. He said that your mother will know you were there because she will see you in her dreams.

I pray that heaven is just as Christopher said it is. I pray that you feel loved and cared for, that you do reach your mother in her dreams. Though your body was not healed, perhaps your soul was, perhaps in dying you have finally reached a place where your soul feels the sense of love that all children deserve.

Every now and then, when I pour myself a glass of soda, I think of you.

"Just a little soda?" I hear you ask.

So here is a toast to you, Eddie: Drink all that your heart desires, and may heaven quench your thirst for life, for love, and for belonging.

↜ POSTSCRIPT

What can be learned from children who, because of trauma or loss, develop their own unique means of asking for love and nurturance? First, we know that traumatized children almost always experience feelings of disempowerment and disconnection from others. Much has been taken from them, and their losses transcend the physical to include emotional losses as well. Children who are sick and homebound have lost their independence and privacy. Children in hospital beds have been robbed of the freedom to run outside, to play with friends, to walk to the corner store, or simply to choose a favorite snack. In addition, the side effects of lifesaving medications—hair loss, reduced energy, low immunity—often cause losses of self-confidence and hope. Friends may not visit often; they may fear they are intruding or may simply not know what to say. When a close friend or family member does offer attention and nurturance, children who have been through medical trauma may avoid intimacy. Avoidance of eye contact, remoteness, and a wish to be left alone may be the ill child's responses to bedside visitors.

Second, we know that emotional recovery for traumatized children depends on their ability to feel powerful in an otherwise out-of-control world. Being able to say, "No, not now," or "Stay and play with me," helps free a child from his sense of powerlessness. Indeed, the language of play is the one language that all children speak fluently and that adults, unfortunately, do not.

Last, we learn that emotional growth comes most often from reconnection with loved ones, or through the creation of new nurturing relationships. Many traumatized children, due to fear, isolation, or lack of truthful information about their condition, become emotionally numb. Their fantasies of their situation may be far worse than the realities that are often kept from them. For the frightened child, providing a sense of belonging is the greatest gift of all. In a world that seems perilous and unpredictable to a child, there is security in feeling loved.

Unfortunately, adults don't always hear when these children ask to belong. Traumatized, scared, or ill children do not speak directly about death, fear, and sadness. Rather, they speak in metaphor and poetry, through play and through tears. Only if we listen closely and with a child's ear will we learn the secret, symbolic language they speak. We must go down on our knees to mine for the gold in a child's words or actions. If we are lucky and patient, we will hear their most heartfelt stories.

Those of us who have dared to enter this land have learned that some of these stories are frightening—they are filled with magical thoughts, confusion, and fear. But the dragons in a child's world can be transformed into kind helpers, and the darkness can be dispelled by the light of acceptance and truth. In the embrace of a loving and patient listener a child can find his path to safety. Only in telling his story can the frightened child eventually befriend his demons and master his experience.

Symbolically or otherwise, as stories are unveiled, wrestled with, and embraced, they need to be told over and over again. It is in the repetition of the tale that the healing begins. As patient listeners, we say, in effect, "Go ahead, I can take it. I am not afraid of your dragons." An angry touch, a frightened glance, or a loud cry may become parts of the secret language being spoken. In allowing the details, unpleasant as they may be, to be reviewed, a frightened child eventually finds a place to put his story. It no longer holds its powerful position as the sole feature of his wounded self. It becomes, rather, another marker on the path of his journey through time.

In listening, we also find that a child's inner explorations, daring as they may be, are carefully structured; his story, with its magic and fire, can only be tolerated by him in small doses. As in listening to a symphony, we await a crescendo, knowing that it will soon be followed by a recapitulation of earlier, quieter, and safer themes. And all the while we listen and lay claim to the child and his fears. We know that one day the storyteller will be healed.

6

A Lesson in Family

One step and two, hold tight, let go.
Twenty and four, hold tight, let go.
I'm nearly there. Let go, let go.
—Cathie Ryan,
Somewhere Along the Road

Dear Rudy,

I came to know you when you were lying in the pediatric intensive care unit. You were in so much pain. You had a fever of 105 and you lay on a cooling pad and asked for a blanket to keep you warm. This was not allowed—a blanket would inhibit the function of the cooling pad. I tried to help you to relax, to feel less cold and to fall asleep. As you lay shivering, I spoke to you of hot things: steam engines, boiler rooms, simmering soup, the sun burning the back of your neck and keeping you warm. As I attempted to guide you to a warmer place, all you said to me was, "Don't stop." I knew I had reached you and made a new friend.

I did not see you for a few weeks after that. You had improved and had gone home to be a twelve-year-old boy with two sisters and one older brother. You were busy watching the Yankees fight their way to the American League championship. With your entire family, you went to Disney World in a wheelchair and took the Magic Kingdom by storm. You danced in Montauk, Long Island, played pranks on your friends at the firehouse where your father volunteered, and eyed your brother as he tried to cheat at poker. You were a Sea Scout, a junior firefighter, an honorary private investigator for the State Police, and a baseball player. You were crowned prince of the children's cancer center, though you always said you preferred to be king.

Then your mother and father were told that your leukemia had recurred and that you would need more rounds of chemotherapy and, eventually, a bone marrow transplant. The search began for a match, your treatments resumed, and, once again, you found yourself in the pediatric intensive care unit. You developed an infection accompanied by fevers and pneumonia that you could not quite shake. On one visit, the pain in your head was so intense that your medication did not to do a thing for you. So I asked you to lie back and go with me on an elevator ride, an imaginary ride down a tall skyscraper that would gently bring you down to the first floor where you could relax and breathe more easily. You found yourself dreaming of a warm, safe place. Gradually, your pain subsided and you were out by the time we reached the sixth floor.

Every day we took another elevator ride. On days when you were thirsty but could not have fluids because of a procedure, we dreamed of dry, arid places. "No oceans, Norm. Don't go there, I'm too thirsty." Some days you were cold, others hot. Some days we traveled more than once because the nurses woke you in the middle of a ride to check your vital signs and take your temperature. Then you would force me to start the ride all over again, from the tenth floor, to the ninth, and all the way back down. Each time we traveled, you fell deeper and deeper into a relaxed, calm, peaceful state.

On Wednesday evenings your brother Billy and I hung out together in my office and played poker. We talked a little about your medical condition, but he would not let me get too "heavy"—it was too difficult for him to concede the possibility of your dying. So we played poker, told jokes, and talked of happier times. He beat me at every hand, until the night we came into your hospital room and included you in our game. Then, as my guide and protector, you pointed out the subtle ways in which Billy might try to cheat.

The night your brother received his first Communion, you were too sick to go to church with the rest of your family. So we agreed to have a little party of our own—nothing big, maybe a movie and a couple of hands of poker. As it became late and neared the time for me to go home, you would not let me leave without yet another elevator ride. And so it went, night after night. With your knowing smile and your loving ways, you made sure that those around you knew they were needed.

Then I learned from the physicians that your pneumonia was getting worse. A bronchoscopy was ruled out because the doctors knew that pneumonia was filling up your lungs and that eventually you would succumb. Your mother asked the oncologist straight out: How long did you have? The answer: seven days.

The decision to bring you home to die was an easy one. But the pain that assaulted your mother and father was devastating. Your father lay on the floor of my office hyperventilating and shivering from the pain of a broken heart. The only thing that could console him was a firm reminder that you were still alive and needed your father.

The next morning the doctors were able to arrange for your discharge. Hospice caregivers would come to your home to provide medical palliation and emotional support. When your ambulance came, I was paged with an urgent message: "Rudy's leaving." I met your family at the helicopter port near the emergency room exit. I promised them I would visit you daily and travel with you in our imaginary elevator down every floor until you relaxed and felt more at ease. You were being wheeled out on a stretcher bed with your mother and father walking behind.

"Hey, Buddy, you're going home. Can I come by to visit you?"

"Yes."

"Can we play poker?" I asked.

"Yes."

"Will you let me beat you?"

"No," you replied.

Your mother and father decided to inform your sisters and brother of everything that was about to happen. But at the age of ten, your little sister Tracy did not believe a word of it.

"Stop crying, everybody," she commanded. "Rudy's not gonna die, okay?"

Your dad sat by quietly, not refuting what she said. He just listened and watched patiently as day by day, hope and truth slowly traded places in her mind.

"How do you spell 'prince,' Mom?" she asked as she watched your mother minister lovingly to your needs. "Mom, I hate you! Why is Dr. Norm here? I'm not talking to any of you."

"Tracy, not now. This isn't a good time."

But Tracy needed to be included. She needed to help you. So I asked her to assist me as we went on an elevator ride. She listened and learned how it went. Hopefully, she would file it away with her memories. And when we gently reached the first floor, I looked around the dimly lit living room where you lay. Everyone except your sister was asleep. She had heard every word and had seen and experienced our ride together. Then she helped you spit out the dried blood that slowly filled your lungs. She sat quietly as you tried to find a comfortable position in which to rest. And you allowed her to stay there and to be needed.

Outside on the front porch, your father sat surrounded by twenty or thirty friends and family members who smoked, laughed, and grieved together. You were so popular, Rudy, and this was your world: volunteer firemen who became your older brothers and teachers; aunts and uncles who played with you and lay down with you whenever you asked; famous wrestlers and football stars who visited you because you loved them. There was never a shortage of love, Rudy, only time.

I sat with your father on that front porch and listened as he slowly began to talk about life. I learned that it was sometimes better not to speak or to ask questions—your father knew what he wanted to say. I just waited and listened. He asked me how he could be so angry at the doctors for not saving your life and yet still love and appreciate them. He told me that he knew you were in trouble when the doctors stopped looking him in the eye when they passed by. He complained about the anorexic teenage girls down the hall from your hospital room, who slowly starved themselves while you struggled to stay alive. He talked about the fundraising events that you loved, the playroom staff, the nurses you liked and disliked. He wanted me to give his thanks to everyone back at the oncology clinic for everything they had done for you. One by one he rehearsed his goodbyes to everyone on the staff. After an hour he thanked me, saying that in thirty-seven years he had never spoken so much to anyone, that it had taken your dying to help him open up.

Your friends all came by the next day, Rudy. Outside your bedroom, scores of people came to honor you. One by one your mother ushered them to your side. Trembling, fearful, and sad, each young boy reached for your hand to shake it. You smiled at every one of them.

"Hey, Mike, thanks for coming," you'd say.

"How ya feelin', Rudy?"

"I'm okay. Just a little tired."

And one boy, Connor, so scared to see how weak and frail you had become, came by with a present. "For me, Connor?" you said, as you slowly pulled the soccer ball out of the bag and smiled. "This is for me to beat you with when I get better."

And Connor said, "Yeah, Rudy. When you get better."

And Connor wrote you a letter that your Aunt Dorothy read to you:

> Dear Rudy,
>
> I know you are very sick. I just want you to know that if you die, can you be my guardian angel? I also want you to know that I am going to miss you. When you die, a part of me will die also. I want you to know that knowing you has been a great pleasure to me. If you die, we will be together again someday in heaven, where, if you do not get better, I can finally beat you in a soccer game.
>
> > Love,
> > A good friend,
> > Connor

And so it continued. Your friends and relatives peeked in to pay you a visit or just to watch you sleep and listen to you breathe.

Your breathing had become more labored and thick as the days passed, and you struggled to clear your airway of the blood in your lungs.

"Spit that shit out!" your uncle demanded. "C'mon, spit that shit out." And with his enthusiasm and your courage, you did "get it all out," and could breathe more easily for a time.

Earlier that day you had taken a ride on a fire truck. You rang the bells, sounded the horn, and asked the drivers to stop in front of your grandpa's house so that you could sit with him and have a club soda. You asked your uncle to buy a bouquet of flowers for your mother.

"Make sure they put two pink roses in it," you ordered.

Pink roses were your mother's favorite. You also asked the nurse to bring a whipped-cream pie for your older brother's birthday. His actual birthday was not for ten more days, but you said you could not wait, you wanted to throw the pie in his face as soon as possible. That night, with your mother standing by to help, your brother offered up his face to your mischievous whim while we took pictures to celebrate.

That night you sat in your big armchair and asked if we could play a game of baseball. I said, "Sure, Rudy," and I created an imaginary field with you on the pitcher's mound.

But you said you wanted to play a game of real baseball. And while your family searched for a video game for you to play with, I whispered in your ear. "Rudy, where do you keep your baseballs?"

You told me to look in the cabinet beneath your desk, and to find your official Don Mattingly autographed ball. I removed it from its protective case and placed it in your right hand.

"Okay, Rudy, let's play!" I shouted.

Your mother ran upstairs and returned with a pitcher's mitt as you assigned players to their positions. You wanted your brother

Billy in right field, Uncle Jim at shortstop, and Aunt Dorothy at first base. Dad was the third-base coach, Maria, your nurse, was the catcher, and the priest at the back of the room played center field. You were on the mound, Rudy, ready to pitch a perfect game.

As your mother cheered, "Batter batter batter batter batter batter," and "Beer here, get your beer here," you raised your frail right hand and threw that ball with all your might.

"Strike one!" I yelled as the ball went straight into Maria's hands.

"Strike two! C'mon, Rudy, you can do it. Strike me out, Buddy. Show me another perfect pitch."

And when you were too tired to throw the ball straight into Maria's hands, and it rolled weakly out of your grip and onto your lap, we called it a foul ball. We played that way for almost half an hour, Rudy. When you tired and drifted off to sleep in your chair, we thought we would end the game. Then, suddenly, gently, you extended your hand to Maria and said, "More. Give me the ball. I'm not done."

You made us all so happy, Rudy. We cheered and applauded your every move. Twenty or more family members and friends stood patiently outside your bedroom door and listened as we laughed and yelled and saluted you as you struck out everyone in the room.

When you were tired, you walked by yourself to your bed and we began another elevator ride to help you go to sleep. I sat there in the darkness by your bed. You lay quietly in your Uncle Jim's big arms, and we rode gently down that elevator. And as we glided slowly and quietly, your breathing became more relaxed.

When the elevator reached the first floor, I reminded you that the doors would open slowly and that you would find yourself in your favorite outdoor place. You were safe and warm there. And you were not alone. "You are here with your Uncle Jim," I said. "You are safe." And then I left you so that you and your uncle could remain together in that safe, warm, very private place.

Hours passed while you and your uncle lay together quietly in your bedroom. He repeated some of my words and assured you of your safety. He whispered in your ear and told you that you were loved. As you lay there, your father summoned me to the basement where he sat, deep in silence. And after several quiet minutes, he asked, "Why won't he die?"

I told him that I truly did not know, but that I believed you were not yet ready. I assured him that you were preparing, but that you would not leave until you were ready. And indeed you were not ready. A few minutes later you sat up in bed and said, "Go get the car."

"Where are we going, Rudy?" I asked.

"We have to go to the store to buy some eggs."

"What do we do with the eggs, Rudy?"

"We have to go to the store to buy some eggs and put them on a blanket and watch them grow," you answered.

"Okay," I said.

"Okay, so let's go," you replied.

"What for?"

"The golden egg. You have to get the golden egg and watch it grow into a golden chicken," you instructed.

And with that, your little sister Tracy ran to the kitchen and came back with two eggs for you. She gently placed one egg on a towel and said, "Here, Rudy. Here on the blanket is the golden egg."

I helped her place the egg in your hand, and I watched as you held it for a short time. Then you slowly fell asleep.

I lay there next to you, and I asked you softly if you wanted to take one last elevator ride.

You said, "Yeah."

And I said, "Hold on to the side rails, Rudy, as this slow-moving elevator gently glides down from the tenth floor to the ninth floor. As it does, you'll feel yourself becoming calmer and more relaxed."

I told you to pay attention to the muscles in your neck and shoulders as this slow-moving elevator glided down to the eighth floor, then the seventh. Your breathing was shallow and soft—no more thickness, no more struggle. As we glided, I told you that the muscles in your stomach, your legs, and your toes were feeling heavier, warmer, and more relaxed. And when we reached the first floor, I told you that the doors were slowly opening. Slowly, ever so slowly. And as you lay there, your face followed my voice as a flower follows the sun. You gently, gradually, turned your face toward the sound of my voice.

"You are here, Rudy. You are healed and whole. Feel how warm and peaceful it is."

There, in silence, you gently lifted your right hand and reached into the darkness for the door. I said, "Go ahead, take it, Rudy. You're safe here, and you are loved."

As you reached, your father lay asleep in the armchair at the foot of your bed, snoring rhythmically as you searched for the door.

I was told that you died a few hours later. I was comforted to know that you were with your mother and father when you passed away, and that you even sat up in a chair moments before you died. I was told that you called out their names, that as you were dying you were told of an "outside Rudy" and an "inside Rudy"—that the outside you was very tired, but that the inside you was strong and full of love and would live on forever. The radio was playing your favorite Spice Girls song. Then you took your last breath and finally, you found the door.

The rest of the story you may not know. Or perhaps you do. You had a fire inspector's full wake and funeral. Three hundred police officers and volunteer firemen stood at attention as your mother and father received the hundreds of friends and family who came by to pay their last respects. There was a sea of white gloves and blue uniforms; rows of men in kilts played the bagpipes. Your father asked me to stay as they said goodbye to your body and closed your casket. He told me that he wanted me to learn from you, that perhaps I could teach others about the pain that a father and mother endure when they lose a child.

I watched as they chose what to place inside your casket, treasured objects to take with you to heaven: your favorite stuffed animal, letters from your sisters and brother, a poem written by a friend, a picture of your family, your baseball mitt, your Nintendo PlayStation, a fishing pole; and a *Playboy* centerfold tucked under your behind. They filled your casket with all the essentials; you would not be in want. Last, your dad placed a crisp twenty-dollar bill between your fingers—your allowance.

Your father asked me to take you on one last elevator ride. "It was the only thing that calmed him," he wept. "And you always seemed to know how to do it better than me. I'd like you to give him one more ride, so that he isn't scared to be buried."

Honored and in awe, at a Mass attended by seventeen hundred family members and friends I guided you down the floors one more time until you gradually arrived at the bottom. I told you that the elevator doors were slowly, slowly opening and that you had arrived in a beautiful, warm, and safe place. I told you that you would be surrounded by warmth, joy, and love forever.

Everyone went back to the firehouse after the interment. They went there to grieve together, to celebrate your life, and to be with you in their sorrow. Your firehouse buddies, your "older brothers," all wore red hats with the inscription "Hats Off to Rudy." They drank and toasted you while your mother played a video of you dancing on the day before you were diagnosed with leukemia, only nine months earlier. Your father asked me if there was a memory pill he could take so that he could forget those joyous days that now broke his heart. I told him there is no pill, that his memories will bring him pain but also, one day, comfort.

ᔁ POSTSCRIPT

What are the lessons that death teaches all families about surviving loss and grief? And how do we, as family members ourselves, stay connected to those we love, long after they have died?

First, we know that death brings about changes not just in each individual family member but in the family system as a whole. The Hebrew Midrash says that "with each life, the world begins anew." It might be added that with each death, the inner world of the family begins anew as well.

Second, we learn that adults and children grieve differently, that the energy each family member uses to resume some semblance of "normal" functioning varies according to age and life experience. In particular, parents' experiences of grief are primarily connected to changes in their sense of self; one's role as a mother or father has been permanently altered. For children, however, grief not only includes changes in family dynamics, it also brings about magical thinking, changes in routines, and fears of abandonment. Children in a grieving family have parents who suddenly may be less emotionally available to them. In addition, the rules that provide order to the home may be altered; events as ordinary as dinner and homework may be forgotten entirely. Secret wishes to "forget the pain," to "move on," to "recapture the past," or simply to "cease living" reverberate in the collective mind of the mourning family searching for resolution.

As adults we learn that our identity as the competent protector of our offspring has been shattered. The promise we made to our newborn child to keep him safe from harm has been broken. We wrestle with feelings of guilt because we have survived; we fear we may not have done enough to save our child. We feel less confident that the decisions we make for our surviving children are the correct ones. The sense that we are in control of our family's destiny is shaken, and our belief in the future is often abandoned. Mothers may find themselves "settling in" to a place that holds an emotion for a few moments, then lets it go, because, as one mourner observed, "Emotions lead to the erroneous belief that we can control or direct the future." Fathers may ruminate over the events leading up to the death of a loved one in an attempt to master the trauma they have been through. This compulsive repetition of memories and events is an expression of our desire to stay connected to our lost love and to regain the power that has been taken from us.

Children, conversely, grieve through changes in behavior— difficulties in school performance, altered sleep and appetite, irritability and poor social relations. Adolescents may feel more comfortable discussing their feelings with someone outside the home for fear that a parent will crumble or be unable to tolerate their pain. They may spend more time with their peer group. Late-night conversations on the computer, sleepover dates, or missed curfews become the adolescent's substitutes for the tears that adults are more willing to shed openly.

Children also come to learn the difference between the death of a sibling and the death of an elder. As one young patient explained:

> Losing a sister is like losing the future. And you don't know what's gonna happen next. But losing a grandparent . . . it's like losing the past. You have your memories and pictures and stuff. For me, it was somehow easier to put the dirt on my grandmother's grave. And walk away.
>
> Nobody put dirt on my sister's grave. They lowered the casket. And we all just stood there. Grandma's death still hasn't affected me as much. I mean, it has . . . but nothing compares to Erica.

We learn that there is a permanent change in the structure and "reality" of the family as a whole. We may feel that our family will never again be complete. As one mourner confessed:

> Traveling is no longer the same . . . it is still shocking to travel with three and not four, and every time I meet someone new I want to tell them that they are not meeting our whole family. Little things like noticing that we don't have as much luggage as we normally do seem to throw me. And I cannot tell you how many times I said to myself, "Oh, Michael would love this, I think I'll buy it," or "Can't wait to tell Michael about this."

We discover that as a family there is an increased sense of vulnerability, sadness, and isolation. Other families seem to function so well; just looking at everyone else's "intact life" leaves us feeling totally on the outside of life. Super Bowl parties, holiday dinners, even backyard barbeques are strained and painful at times. When the surviving children are of a different gender than that of the deceased child, mother-daughter and father-son relationships may take on new energy. We discover that the child who is gone may have provided a buffer against the normal tensions that arise in all growing families. As one mourner expressed it:

> I feel like my daughter and my husband gang up on me a lot. This spills over to what is happening in general, for developmentally, my daughter is at the point where she is pulling away from me. The differences between her and Sean are gender-based as well as personality-based. I could never do anything to embarrass Sean. The goofier I was, the more he laughed. My daughter is much more uptight, and is always forbidding me to do something. Maybe it's a girl thing, I understand. But it just intensifies my son's absence.

For some, changes in the family structure cause changes in the marital relationship. We may feel estranged or removed from our spouse for a time as each of us retreats to his or her private place of grieving. As spouses, we see that women and men grieve differently. We realize that men are "do-ers": they check under the hood of the car, fix the grill, and make sure there is money in the bank. This is often a man's way of surviving the pain of loss, and is an important means of showing love. Women are more likely to define themselves as "be-ers": they allow grief to overtake them. This level of vulnerability may be seen by some men as a weakness, and as a consequence a sense of estrangement or discord may develop in a marriage. As one mother remarked:

> To use the metaphor of internal seasons, it seems that I really haven't been out of winter since my son's diagnosis. Or, quite probably, I may have spent most of my life in winter, and his suffering and death plunged me into the deepest, darkest winter yet endured. But my husband doesn't seem to be with me in that darkness. He won't read the books I bring home, and he won't come to therapy. He has his friends, and his work, but he is very private in his pain for our son.

Through all the trials and changes we endure as a family, we eventually learn that there is indeed personal and familial growth through grief. Varied though our separate experiences of grief may be, as mothers, fathers, and children we begin to redefine the family unit until we achieve a new reality. Together we see how fragile life is, and we take each other more seriously than we used to. We speak of increased strength; we say that our family "can make it" and that "There is nothing we can't handle after this." We have an increased sense of one another's pain and suffering, and a greater awareness that all families have their sorrows. Moreover, when siblings have been a part of the loved one's dying process, the family achieves a quiet understanding that "Together we did all that we could."

Slowly we reengage in the activities of the living—in fussing over the menu for Thanksgiving dinner, in cooking a beautiful meal, in welcoming moments of joy back into our home. If we are lucky, we realize that our family, and each individual member in it, has received the absolute best from us, even in the worst of times.

7

A Lesson in Believing

Man can try to name love, showering upon it all the names at his command, and still he will involve himself in endless self-deceptions. If he possesses a grain of wisdom, he will lay down his arms and name the unknown by the more unknown . . . by the name of God.

—Carl Jung

Dear Vincenzo,

It is said that everything in the world is a reflection of our own features. If this is so, the mirror of your life shines in my memory with rays of goodness, hope, and holiness. You were a religious young man, and your faith in God carried you through days of pain and sorrow that not even your mother's love could mend. You were a gifted artist and, early in your life, a talented soccer player. But your tumor had affected your ability to perform in these areas and, as the years wore on, the damage to your brain became increasingly obvious. But through it all, your faith in God and your belief in His miracles remained the one unchanging backdrop to your lonely life. Your faith would never be shaken by the earthly, mortal trials that you were forced, or perhaps had even chosen, to endure.

You were sad so much of the time. Sometimes I saw you walking through the halls of the hospital, unaware that you were being watched. You were deep in thought and your face was pale and distorted—the long waves of your unruly hair could not hide the longing in your soul.

You were the third son in a family of four boys. Your younger brother, no longer a little child himself, would grow to outrun you on the soccer field and outshine you with the girls. Your Sicilian parents were averse to your having friends outside the family, so you spent much of your time alone, painting, drawing, or reading the Bible. I remember how, in broken English, your mother would thank me for spending time with you. "Grazie per tu amicizia," she would say. And what she could not say with words, she made known through smiles of gratitude and pride. Pride that her son had a doctor for a friend. Pride that, after everything you had lost, you still commanded love and respect.

It was your mother who supported your goal to apply to, and eventually attend, the School of Visual Arts. But since you were too afraid to travel alone by train to your classes in the city, your father accompanied you. For days he sat in the back of the classroom and watched as you tried to learn the techniques of cartoon illustration and portrait painting. And after only three weeks of venturing outside your small world, you stopped attending those classes. Was it because you were uncomfortable as he watched? Or was it that you found it too painful to discover how impaired you had become as your cancer had grown? How I wished for you the things that life had offered me when I was your age: friendship, music, and the promise of a future.

But your childhood was different. You knew on some deep level that your body would eventually betray you—your father told me how, long before you were diagnosed, you spent summer nights drawing self-portraits that pinpointed the exact location of your tumor. And how instead of riding your bicycle to a ball field after school, or playing with peers in the park, you sat alone with the Bible, reading about God's love and His promise of eternal life.

Months turned into years, and still you suffered through surgeries and chemotherapy, radiation and doctors' visits. Years turned quickly into a lifetime of medicine and prayers, and a dawning awareness of your eventual demise.

You grew weak and pale and less able to move about without your brother's help or the aid of a wheelchair. I remember how your family tried to keep you out of the hospital as much as possible. Always later than the doctors wished, your father could be seen wheeling you down the long hallways where you had once walked. Your face was sad, and your hair—your symbol of strength and protection—had been stripped away by your chemotherapy. Like Samson, weakened and betrayed, the world you leaned upon was coming down.

The decision to care for you through hospice at home was equally difficult. Your father, unaccustomed to allowing strangers into his home, had to reckon with the social worker and her pleas to allow the nurses to come and take care of you. It was the only way you could receive the medicines you needed to ease your pain and still remain at home with those you loved. I visited daily, undaunted by the strict rules that ran your household. What I saw was a young man afraid and alone, with only his brothers for friends. So with patience and curiosity, I learned the language and the customs I needed to know in order to sit with you and your family in your home.

"Dr. Norman!" your older brother would call to me as I approached your front stoop each evening after work. Nightly we sat at the small round table in the middle of your kitchen, drinking thick black coffee and eating biscotti.

"Fango," I used to call it. "Mud."

"This is the way we used to drink it in Italy," your brother laughed. "My father's country."

We talked for a while, your brother and I, about his feelings and his fears for you as you lay sleeping on the couch in the next room. Your mother tried to teach me to speak Italian, and your brother would shyly ask me if there was anything special I wanted from the market. Finally, after exchanging warm words and quiet laughter with them, I entered the living room where you lay with your IV pole standing stalwartly at your side. Attached to it was a clear bag of saline solution. I remember how painful it was to see you lying quietly by the light of the television, with only time and salt water keeping you with us.

I found myself drawn to those dark winter nights at your bedside. Sometimes you asked me about my work at the hospital, about my family and friends. Sometimes you told me of the years in your life when you were hale and whole. You proudly showed me the artwork and soccer trophies that adorned the small breakfront in the living room, where you spent your days. But mostly we read together from the Bible. And when you grew too weak to read along with me, you led me to the passages you wished to hear. There, by the dim light of the muted television in the corner, we sat and read. We read from the Letter of Paul to the Romans, and from the Gospels of Luke and John.

"Luke 8:43," you instructed. "Let's start there tonight."

And a woman having an issue of blood twelve years, which had spent all her living upon physicians, neither could be healed of any, came behind him *and touched the border of his garment: and immediately her issue of blood stanched.*

And Jesus said, Who touched me? When all denied, Peter and they that were with him said, Master the multitude throng thee and press thee, *and sayest thou, Who touched me?*

When I looked over at you, your eyes were closed. I did not know if you were asleep or simply deep in thought. Then, after a momentary pause in my reading, you opened your eyes. You smiled at me and asked me to read on.

And Jesus said, Somebody hath touched me: for I perceive that virtue is gone out of me.

And when the woman saw that she was not hid, she came trembling, and falling down before him, she declared unto him before all the people for what cause she had touched him, and how she was healed immediately. And he said unto her, Daughter, be of good comfort: thy faith hath made thee whole; go in peace.

While he yet spake, there cometh one from the ruler of the synagogue's house *saying to him, Thy daughter is dead; trouble not the Master. But when Jesus heard* it, *he answered him, saying, Fear not: believe only, and she shall be made whole.*

"Do you believe?" you asked me.

"Do I believe what, Vincenzo?"

"Do you believe that Jesus was able to heal the sick?"

"I don't know, Vincenzo," I replied. "This is all very new to me." You knew that I was born and raised a Jew, and that reading the New Testament was, for me, an opening into a new way of believing.

"Please promise me that you will read His words. I believe that God heals the sick, and I want you to believe also."

Why was it so important to you, Vincenzo, that I be a believer? Why did you struggle so long and so hard to "save me," as you put it? Were you afraid that God would not heal you? Were you afraid that I lived in darkness? Or were you afraid that, in order to be received into heaven, you needed to save me first?

In my Father's house are many mansions: if it *were not* so, *I would have told you. I go to prepare a place for you.*

And if I go and prepare a place for you, I will come again and receive you unto myself; that where I am, there *ye may be also. And whither I go ye know, and the way ye know.*

I remember how you cried with joy when you saw me enter your living room one night with my own copy of the New Testament. I ask myself now if I misled you. It's true that I wanted to learn more about your religion in order to understand you better. Yet how far was I capable of walking for a closer glimpse of your world of fear and awe?

Night after night I read to you. And as I read the precious words of your immortal teachers, I came to know you better, and I came to know your God through your frightened, believing eyes.

The passage that I read to you most often was Romans 6:23: *For the wages of sin* is *death; but the gift of God* is *eternal life through Jesus Christ our Lord.* Indeed, across the room from where you lay dying, this verse was scribbled on a piece of pale construction paper and hung low on the living room wall so that you could see it.

What was your sin, Vincenzo? What was it that you believed you did wrong? Looking back now, I remember the sound of your struggle. The horrible shrieks that I heard as I stood outside your father's house waiting to be let in. From the stoop where I sat, I became aware of your conflict:

"It's not true! It is not true! I am not!" you cried out as you lay in the darkness.

"Get out, get out!" you yelled at your mother, using words that would later cause you shame.

These were not your ways when you were well, Vincenzo. We all knew this and forgave you. Was this the morphine talking? Were you wrestling with your God? Or with your demons? I regret that I will never know what it was that hurt you so. But I stood by your side and tried to show you that a friend remains true, even in times of pain and sorrow. On the nights that you asked, even begged, that I not enter your room, I did as you asked. Were you afraid of the feelings that friendship and love engendered in you? Were you frightened that you would not be received by God because you had not saved me? Were you angry at him for your fate? Or did the darkness of your stale and lonely room confuse you?

Shortly thereafter you were transferred to the hospital. It was your father's request that you receive a blood transfusion—red cells for strength and platelets for clotting. But you would not return home after that visit. Your mother and father sat patiently at your bedside as your breathing became more labored and shallow. They remained by your side, read from your Bible, and awaited God's miracle. With certainty your mother told all who came to your bed that you would be healed. "God will come to us and show us his miracle. God will heal him," she said.

I remember when I told her that there was nothing more the doctors could offer you. She smiled and, not unkindly, asked me if I believed in the Resurrection. I struggled with my answer:

"Your son taught me much about God's love and his will," I said. Then I lowered my head and gently told her that what was most important was how deeply she believed in the Resurrection. But she knew that, after all those long weeks at your bedside, reading and learning and sharing with you, I still did not believe. And she said to me, "Then you cannot help us any longer."

Sadly, I sat on the floor next to your bed while your mother read the Bible and your father watched you. Together we sat in that quiet hospital room. "Peaceful. So peaceful," I found myself thinking.

As your breath became increasingly weak and shallow, it took you longer to exhale. Finally, you took one last breath. I looked over at your mother, and we shared a knowing glance. But your father did not understand what had happened. He looked at me with panic in his eyes. His face, his whole being, demanded that I do something. But I sat there motionless, in awe of your faith and of God's will for you.

Your mother took your father by the hand and guided him to your bed where together they closed your eyes. Your mother embraced me. She held me in her arms and glorified God's name. "I told you that God would perform a miracle," she said. "I told you that He would heal my boy. And He has. For now my son is with God. He is finally healed."

And so, my dear friend, here I sit with many prayers in my heart. I pray that you are whole again and in a weightless world filled with wonder and glory. I pray that He was there at your arrival; that with outstretched arms and radiant with eternal love, He ushered you into his kingdom.

As for me, well, I have kept my promise, Vincenzo. I read from the Bible that you loved so, and I continue my journey in believing. I can truthfully say I believe that no matter what your faith, love heals, and that all who love are saved.

~ POSTSCRIPT

What can be said about the power of belief in the healing process? We know that without faith, without the sacred and the spiritual in our lives, our actions lack meaning. We must ask ourselves if there can truly be healing without a belief in the unknown, the unnameable. Larry Dossey, in *Healing Words: The Power of Prayer and the Practice of Medicine*, asserts that to acknowledge the mystery of prayer and faith leads to a glorious conclusion: that to believe *is* to be healed. He states that this mystery is ineradicable. "Try as we might, we shall not be able to abolish it." In addition, Carl Jung suggested that in numinous experiences, we find release from our pathology. The disease itself takes on a spiritual character, he claims.

As mourners we wake each day to constant reminders of our humanness: we prepare lunch for our children; we pay the overdue bills; we find ourselves involved in the "stuff" of this world. But when darkness falls and we are alone with our pain, it is God, or the rituals of our faith, to which we most often turn. Some of us find solace in a community of believers, and we look to spiritual leaders for guidance and direction. We discover that the work of life requires endurance, persistence, and a determined effort to "make it to the finish line." Beneath this determination is the undying belief that our God or our loved one will be there to greet us when we arrive. For most of us there is no surviving grief without faith.

In our times of sorrow, the Bible is the starting point of our search for meaning. For in searching for the meaning behind our human pain, we discover that we are unable to accept a world without some comforting force. As Viktor Frankl has said, "Meaning is something to be found, not given. Man cannot invent it, but discover it." We are left with the difficult task of trying to understand the reasons for life's pain, says Irvin Yalom, all the while knowing that the answers may lie in a dimension beyond our comprehension. Many of us find comfort in relinquishing this task by blindly accepting God's will. "God had a plan for my loved one," we hear mourners say. "It is faith that brought me through my pain in the past, and it will sustain me now."

Others among us refuse to accept that our fate, with all its suffering, has been preordained. Instead we are left to face an indifferent, disordered world. We feel that our prayers have been ignored, that there is no reason to believe anymore. "What kind of God lets this happen?" we ask. The answer is unclear; and in the absence of meaning or pattern, we feel dissatisfied and helpless. But without the belief that we can decipher meaning in suffering, we rob ourselves of the chance to gain mastery over our pain. Moreover, if we believe that our groping for meaning has been in vain, then, as Viktor Frankl says, we may lose the ability to successfully cope with suffering.

Regardless of our religion, it is faith that provides us with direction and purpose. We know that the journey through sorrow is arduous; it is filled with pain and uncertainty. But when we believe, we discover that we do not walk this path alone, and that our chances of survival are much improved. In our search for meaning, we are strengthened by the hope that, eventually, our questions will be answered in a distant, spiritual place, where all is made right and we are no longer "wronged." Most important, we know that faith, and the love it teaches, will save us and bring us to a place where our loved ones are whole and we are healed as well.

8

A Lesson in Truth

Tomorrow we will run faster, stretch out our arms farther, and so . . . we
beat on, boats against the current, borne ceaselessly into the past.
— *F. Scott Fitzgerald, The Great Gatsby*

Dear Danny,

We all stand at the edge of life and valiantly face what lies ahead.
We follow in the footsteps of our parents, our teachers, and our heroes at the same time that we struggle to find our own path, to
reach a place that is new and untrammeled. And even as we arrive
in that new place, we often discover that we've been there before.
We learn that projections from the past are being replayed in the
present, like tapes of our earlier, more primitive selves. Is this the
natural course of a life? Do all of us, families and individuals alike,
unknowingly carry a map through the generations that guides us
back to a place where we have already been? These are the ques-

tions that you inspire. For your path through illness and despair seemed almost predetermined. The choices that your family made in their care of you seemed, not unkindly, to be part of an unconscious script written years before you were born.

You were the second son of a young couple—a middle child, a "gift from God," as your mother called you. Your place in the family was filled with contradiction and challenge: you were born blonde, your brothers brunette. You were quiet, slow, and often afraid. Your brothers were loud, daring, and successful. You were your mother's favorite child, your father's private heartache, and your brothers' secret burden.

"My son is different," your mother would say. "He's a nerd, a retard. He's really not, but for years this is what I have been told. My son the retard," she silently chanted. "But he is the one thing I did right."

My friendship with you was, for me, one of the gifts that life provides without warning or preparation. I had not planned to love you. Every time you passed me in the long corridors of the hospital, you said with a soft smile, "Hello, Dr. Norm." But often I didn't respond; I was not always aware of you as you walked by. Yet, somehow, with persistence and determination, your hellos became a part of the rhythm of my day. And as the days passed, I began to wonder about you, this quiet sixteen-year-old with a slight limp and a soft slur in his speech. Did I see you as others saw you? Was your mother right, that your outer layer of gracelessness masked a hunger for friendship?

Perhaps this is what prevented me from befriending you early on in your cancer journey. Perhaps I was too caught up in the romance of healing to see the path of pain and truth that lay before you. But when the doctors gathered to discuss the gravity of your condition, when I was told that your disease had progressed rapidly, I was compelled to make the acquaintance of the boy behind the soft smile.

Behind closed doors, the oncology team struggled with the few medical options still available to you. More chemotherapy would ravage your already weakened body; yet without it, remission could not be achieved. And without remission, you could not receive the bone marrow transplant that was believed to be your best chance for survival.

"Someone is going to have to tell the parents," one doctor said. "Someone should be there to help this family understand that this is the end."

I approached your bedside knowing things that had significantly tipped the balance of our new friendship. You were dying. You were unaware of this, however. You wanted to talk about the DVDs that were sold in the hospital gift shop. You were occupied with the stuff of this life: books, video games, television shows. And there in the world of the living we stayed, two new friends talking about our favorite TV shows and our likes and dislikes. When I eventually turned to leave, you looked up at me and said, "I like Norman." You spoke about me in the third person, as if someone else were there with us. In this way our relationship began. And in that first conversation I finally saw the grace in your tortured body.

As I walked away from your room, I noticed your mother in the hospital corridor, waiting for me by the water fountain. This location would eventually become our standard meeting point; it was a resting place from the war we were waging as well as a staging area for the difficult decisions that lay ahead.

"My son is dying," she began. "I know that. I always asked the doctors to tell me when we'd hit the brick wall. And they told me today that we can't get him back into the bone marrow unit. They can't look me in the eye anymore. I know we're hitting the brick wall, and I'm ready for it. I'm straight with people. You already know that about me. I always dreaded the day when the doctors couldn't look us straight in the eye. And now they can't.

"We asked Danny's doctors how they planned to tell him. They said not to tell him anything, that he'll figure it out on his own. When we asked them why, they said that they felt he might lose hope if he knew, and then give up. They said it might make him die sooner.

"I have listened to doctors all of my life, Norman," your mother said. "So I am trying to listen to them now. But it makes no sense to me. I have always been honest with my son. We always stressed the truth. I was the one who told him he had cancer in the first place. I told him that he had to have a bone marrow transplant. I told him that it had failed and that he'd relapsed. And now that he is dying I'm not supposed to let him know? How can I do that?"

I listened in silence. Your mother had a story to tell and was in need of a witness; she needed to testify to your life and to declare the truth—that you were not getting better. She was not accustomed to living under a veil of hope, which seemed too much like a lie to her now. She raised you to be proud and honest, and she was determined to continue to teach you these lessons, even as you lay dying.

"I have three sons," she continued. "Danny's two brothers have everything. They're good-looking, athletic. They're smart. But Danny's a retard. Not really, you know. But that's all I ever heard from his classmates. And the thing that really hurts is that he never had a friend. He gets along with adults. They all love him, because they see the real Danny, the one I love. But kids can be mean. And they were. And Danny used to come to me and tell me what they all called him, what they said to him.

"I was his friend. I was his best friend. I always said to him: 'You're my best friend, Danny. Don't you give up, Danny. You keep trying; try hard for me. 'Cause I need you, 'cause I can't make it without you, Danny. You're all I've got.'"

Your mother spoke urgently. She passed compulsively through the stages of your short life. She was lost in memories but made no apologies. Then she said, "I told the whole family. His brothers know. They look at him and lie to him. Danny asks them when he'll be able to go back into the bone marrow unit. We all say, 'Maybe next week.' How can we go on like this? I want him to know. I just don't know how to tell him. I was hoping that he had given you an indication in your talks that he knew he was dying."

I told her that you had not said anything that led me to believe you were aware of your fate. But I assured her that I would visit you daily, and that I would listen closely to the stories you told. I told her that, as a witness to your journey, I hoped to hear messages in your stories—messages about your wishes and fears. And you did have stories to tell, in part because yours was a life lived mostly on the sidelines. You had seen the way the game was played, and you had much to say about the rules and how they needed to change. And when I arrived at your bedside early the following morning, your messages had begun:

"How are you feeling, Buddy?" I asked.

"You have a funeral to go to?" you responded.

"No. What?"

"You have a funeral to go to?" you repeated.

"No, Buddy," I said. "How are you feeling?"

"Oh," you answered. "I thought you said you had a funeral to go to."

"No," I assured you.

"Oh . . . good. I would be sad if you had to go to a funeral."
Then you cried.

Looking back, I realize now how ready you were to tell your
story, and that you had chosen me as your translator. I stood there
at your side, awestruck by your determination. In the darkness of
that heavy hospital room you held tight to the oxygen tube that
supplied you with air. You lay back in your bed and, using that tube
as a microphone, you said the following words to me:

"I made a cake."

"You made a cake," I repeated.

"Yeah."

"I didn't know you could cook."

"Yeah," you answered.

"Who's it for?" I asked.

"For me."

"What's the occasion?"

"I don't know," you cried.

"What's written on the cake?"

"For Danny only," you said.

"Just for you?"

"Yeah."

"What flavor is it?" I asked. "Chocolate? Strawberry?"

"It's chocolate and vanilla."

"Does it have candles on it?"

"Yes."

"How many?" I asked.

"A lot."

"Who can eat the cake?"

"Nobody. Only me . . . and you."

And at that moment I knew that I had reached you. Together we would talk in metaphor, and hopefully, if I followed you carefully enough, I would learn the message that you wanted your family to hear.

"You and me, Danny?"

"Yeah," you replied. "Danny and Norman. But you better get there in time."

"What's the rush?" I asked.

"It may not be there when you get there," you answered.

"Why not?"

"I may eat it all. And I don't want to eat it all," you said.

"Where's there, Danny? Where are we?"

"My house. It's in my house. I live there. I've gotta clean up a lot of things. I left a mess."

"You left a mess?"

"Yeah."

"Where?"

"In the kitchen. I've gotta clean things up. I left the stove on."

"How can I help you clean up?" I asked. "Is there a way I can help?"

At that very moment, in the darkness of that sad room, in the middle of your story, the nurses entered. With their medicine carts loudly preceding them, they turned on the overhead lights and pulled open the blinds.

"Time to take your vitals," your nurse announced.

I was yanked out of a faintly glowing dream into the naked, screaming glare of reality. "Can this wait until later?" I urged.

"Afraid not," the nurse answered. She had her own job to do.

I stood there, confused at the paradox of your healing: your body was failing you, this we all knew; but your spirit grew stronger with every dying breath. You had a story to tell, a message to convey, and your soul was learning to transcend corporeal things. I waited until the nurses left your room. Then I closed the blinds, turned off the lights, and watched as you repositioned yourself into the curves of your bed.

"Where were we?" you asked.

With a smile, I reminded you of where we had left off. Even now, as I retell your story, I marvel at your resolve. You had work to do, and you would not allow the things of this world to stop you from completing it.

"We were in the kitchen," I smiled. "You told me to hurry or I might not make it."

"Oh yeah. You're there," you answered.

"I'm there?"

"Yeah. And there's a beautiful woman. She's attracted to me."

"She finds you attractive, Danny?" I repeated. I was happy that you dreamed of being desired and loved.

"And she finds you attractive. She likes you," you added.

"Likes me?" I asked.

"Yes. She's attracted to you. She wants to marry you. I am nice to you. I give her to you. I let you have her."

"Why, Danny?"

"Because she likes you and you like her."

Was this your way of asking me to take care of your mother? Were you trying to tell me something about your parents' marriage? Or were you summoning dreams of an unlived future while caught in an unconscious oedipal struggle? I knew that you were trying to tell me about "your mess," so I sat there in silence, hoping to make sense of it all.

"I'm tired now, Norman. Maybe we can talk some more tomorrow," you said.

"Okay, Danny. Tomorrow. You sleep well now."

I walked out of that dark room and into the colorful hallway. Passing by the water fountain, I saw your mother, alone and deep in thought. Looking up at me, she said: "I spoke to the doctors. We both did, my husband and me." I waited as she struggled to compose the words that would explain her fears, her plan.

"We told them that we are very uncomfortable about not telling Danny that he is dying," she offered. "And the doctor said that this was a critical night for Danny, and that we'll know soon if he'll make it. He urged us not to say anything in the next twenty-four hours. But I can't. I want Danny to know. Maybe he'd have a last wish. I know my son, he wouldn't want a trip. He's not that kind of kid. He'd want to go home. But maybe he wants to say something to us, and we won't give him a chance. We've decided to tell him tonight."

Carefully I told her about the conversation you and I had in your hospital room. Word for word I told her your story of the cake and of the mess you had left behind. From deep within her broken heart, in a place where joy and sorrow exist quietly side by side, your mother smiled and lowered her head. "He knows," she cried. "You see, he knows and he wants to talk about it. He left a mess and he wants to talk about it."

Relieved of the burden that no mother is prepared to carry, she discussed her plan with me:

"We won't say, 'Danny, you're dying.' We decided that we'll tell him that he can't get back into the bone marrow unit. We'll tell him that there are medicines to try, but not a transplant. And if he asks, 'Will I die?' we will say, 'You may die, Danny. Yes, you may die.'"

And then, with generosity and gratitude, your mother looked up at me with tears in her eyes. "Thank you," she said. "Thank you for talking to my son. You know how to talk to him and how to comfort him. And I can't thank you enough for that. He really likes you. He talks about Norman all the time. He told me that you're his friend. Thank you."

The next morning you sat up in your bed and, using your oxygen tube as your microphone again, you gave your mother instructions. You said, "Be nicer to Grandma. You better be nicer to people, Ma. You're not nice to people."

Warmed by your commitment to the world, she smiled at you and said, "Yes, Danny. Yes, I will be nicer to her."

You told your mother that you were leaving.

She asked you, "Where are you going?"

You said that you didn't know, but there were a lot of people there. People you didn't know yet.

Your mother told you to go to them.

You told her that you were afraid, that you didn't know them. You asked her if she could go with you.

She told you that she could not.

You asked her why.

And she said, "Because it is not my time yet."

"Why is it my time, Mama?"

"I don't know, Danny. I don't know."

Slowly I approached your bedside. "Danny, do you want to continue with our story?"

"Yeah," you replied.

Hoping that I would come to understand your fears more clearly, I asked, "Do you remember that yesterday you told me that you had made a cake?"

"Yeah."

"And you said that you left a mess?"

"Yeah."

"Is there any mess left now?" I gently asked.

"You failed," you answered.

"I failed?"

"Yeah. You were too late. There's only a little left. Under the chairs. There's just a little left," you said.

What was left? I wondered. What of your "mess" remained unfinished? Were you worried about your mother and father? Or was there something more you were asking me to decipher?

"Remember how you gave me your girlfriend?" I asked you.

"Yes."

"What happens next?"

"You get married. You're marrying her," you answered. And then, with your hand still on the "microphone" you loved to hold, you instructed me to buy her a card.

"What kind of card, Danny?"

"Any card."

"What should the card say?"

"Nothing."

"What is it for?"

"You'll figure it out."

Then the nurses arrived again, this time to give you a dose of medicine to calm you. They told me to hurry—the medicine they were about to give you would make you sleepy. But I did not go. I was afraid to leave you there.

When the nurses finally left, I asked, "Should I go now?"

"No," you said. "It's too late."

"It's too late?"

"Yeah."

"What happened?"

"She left you."

"She left me?" I replied quietly.

"She's very angry," you went on.

"What did I do?"

"You never come home. You're always working. You're not home for dinner," you explained.

"How can I change things, Danny?"

"She needs you," was your reply.

"What does she need?"

"She needs you to comfort her."

And then you drifted off to sleep as the medicine took effect. Sleep. Quiet. Rest from the battle. I looked up and found myself in the dark room of your disrepair. The rhythm of your shallow breathing and the soft puff of air in the tube in your hand filled the room with sorrow.

In that moment I understood what it was you were trying to say to me. I understood your fears for your lonely mother, who, at the end of each tired day, waited for your father to comfort and protect her. But you were her only true friend, Danny. It was always you and Mom. And now that you were leaving, you knew she would need a new best friend.

So young, I thought. And yet you had so much to say. And even as you lay dying, you were intent on fixing what you could.

Later that evening, I found your father sitting by your side. I sat down next to him and quietly told him about your stories, about the cake, and about "my wife." I spoke of the symbols you had created in your effort to explain what was in your heart.

"It's a terrible thing to watch a loved one die," your father responded.

"Have you ever lost someone close to you before?" I asked.

"Yes. My father," he said. "I was Danny's age. I had come home from school and the house was filled with relatives. But no one told me what was wrong. They only told me to go up to my room and to wait," he explained. "And I remember how I listened at the crack of my door to what they were saying in the kitchen below. There were people crying and I heard someone ask, 'How do we tell Joseph?' And I knew then that my father had died. I figured it out myself. There, alone in my room."

"So you never had a chance to say goodbye to him?"

"No. I went off to school and never saw him again," he cried. "And now, I have to say goodbye to my son. And I can't do it. I just can't."

Even as your mother stood on one side of your bed and lovingly whispered in your ear, "Go. Go to Grandma," your father stood on the other side and whispered, "Stay. Don't leave me, son. Don't disobey me." And there, caught in the middle of a human struggle you had witnessed all your life, you lay breathing ever more slowly.

The doctors informed your father that it was time to gather the family. "Tonight may be the night," they said.

"How do I let him go?" your father asked me. "What should I say?"

I could not answer. I merely looked at him and, with tears in my eyes, reminded him of what he had said to me earlier that afternoon. "You told me today that when you were Danny's age, your father died and you never had the chance to say goodbye. You told me that you never learned how a son says goodbye to a father," I said.

"Yes," he said.

"But what you were also saying is that you never learned how a father says goodbye to a son."

"My father said goodbye to me," he answered. "He said goodbye every morning when he went to work."

"Yes," I said. "But he didn't say goodbye when it mattered the most."

Your father stood there as if turned to stone. He pondered what I had said, then quietly turned and walked away.

Between one moment and the next, we age a lifetime. Later that same day, your mother came to me crying. "It's a miracle," she said. "I don't know what you told him, but he did it. My husband leaned over and whispered into Danny's ear, 'Go. Go to Grandma. I'm letting you go now.' He cried and kissed Danny, and then he came over to Danny's brothers and hugged them. In all my life I've never seen him hug his sons. Come," she urged. "Come and see."

Your whole family surrounded your bed as I entered that solemn room. "Your buddy's here, Danny. Norm's here," your mother said. But you did not look at me. Your eyes passed right over me as you scanned the faces in the room. Did you see me there, Danny? Were you aware of but no longer in need of my presence? Were you, as I had hoped, finished telling your stories?

I leaned over and whispered in your ear, "I'm leaving now, Danny. Good job. You did a good job cleaning up your mess." Then I left you.

I was told you died soon thereafter. I was told you were with your mother and father and your two brothers. Your father held your mother as you left this world; and your mother looked toward the ceiling and said, "Thank you. Thank you."

And now I sit here thinking of all that you taught me about your parents and your broken world. I think of how every one of us has a story to tell, and that with the help of loved ones, we can finish our story and say the necessary words of goodbye; we can finally clean up the mess we are leaving behind.

So I thank you, Danny. I thank you for choosing me to listen. I thank you for entrusting me with the symbolism and urgency of your message. And I thank you for showing us how to live without you. Our memories and our faith serve as the glue that binds the fragments of our lives together. And your message of love and restoration, this too will carry us forward. For we all have a mess to clean up, and I pray that we do it as gracefully and as beautifully as you did.

⌁ POSTSCRIPT

One of the most difficult tasks of living, particularly for those who have witnessed the suffering of a loved one, is to identify the critical events from a vast collection of human experience that, when put together, tell the honest story of a life well lived. Whether the story has defeat, sorrow, or redemption as its theme, it is truth that must be the long-range goal. Truth gives us a chance to understand and, eventually, to end the unconscious repetition of mistakes made earlier in our lives, and even in previous generations. Last, it is truth that ensures a place in history for our loved ones who have died.

Danny's story is an example of how, in speaking truthfully and listening carefully, the lessons that the dying convey can help the living to heal. As the middle child in his family, Danny witnessed patterns of behavior that affected all its members. Furthermore, his physical challenges caused him to spend a great deal of time with his mother. In the process, and perhaps *because* of this process, he grew to understand what was broken in her world, and he tried to the very end of his life to fix it. But Danny's father, who struggled with untruthful messages from his own past, remained trapped in an intergenerational conflict that he played out unconsciously in the present. It was Danny's mother who encouraged the truth. Danny was dying, and she knew that she could not endure this painful process without honoring the very thing that would save her family, even if it could no longer save Danny: the truth.

As mourners we know there is little dignity in dying. We watch as our loved one is transformed by illness into a nearly unrecognizable version of himself. Some of us visit less often as the dying process ensues; it is too difficult to see our beloved like this, we hear ourselves say. Others find that they are unable to leave their loved one's side. They remain there as day turns to night and as weeks turn to months.

When death occurs suddenly and without warning, we recognize the importance of the farewell that has been stolen from us. But when we are given the grace of a warning, and we can say truthfully to our beloved, "I know you are dying," we redefine the healing process. We offer dignity where there was none before. We provide our loved one with the chance to say the necessary words of goodbye, and we give ourselves and our families the chance to say goodbye as well. In speaking truthfully we discover that there are still messages to be deciphered and lessons to be learned. We discover that surviving this loss and living a meaningful life after the farewell is truly possible. For although we cannot heal a body at the end of its life, we *can* heal a family and a future that is yet to be lived.

9

A Lesson in Acceptance

And if the earthly no longer knows your name,
whisper to the silent earth: I'm flowing.
To the flashing water say: I am
—Rainer Maria Rilke

Dear Julio,

It has been said that night is never dark enough to hide us from our own reflection; that the thing we fear most is, "in its deepest being," ours to wrestle with and to love. These are the lessons that your journey through cancer taught me. Through all the trials you endured on your path from sickness to health and to sickness again, you remained undaunted and ever aware. Through prayers and poems, you revealed your secret strength—at sixteen, you were already a grown man battling your second round of leukemia. You hoped to achieve remission from your disease so that you could receive a bone marrow transplant.

The day I met you, you told me that you were a poet. You stood quietly before me, having just learned the grave news of your medical condition. Your dark, haunting eyes seemed to reveal that you knew, right from the start, what your fate would be. You were quiet much of the time; you shared your thoughts and feelings cautiously and only after careful consideration within a deep, safe place inside. You excelled in your classes at school. You spent long hours writing and drawing about your fears while your peers were out drinking and laughing their way through theirs. Your older sister had just started college in New England, leaving only you and your grandmother in the small apartment you shared in Queens. Your mother visited you several times each month, but her work demanded that she be away much of the time. And so, accompanied by your aging grandmother, you arrived quietly for each clinic visit, ready for another day of medicine and the fading promise of a miracle.

Grandma Rosa, as all of the doctors and nurses came to call her, often brought fresh baked goods and other delicious gifts from her kitchen. We looked forward to those visits, for your sweet conversation was a perfect complement to your grandmother's homemade bread. And whatever medicines the clinic lacked for our everyday aches and pains, your grandmother supplied in one of her recipes from the old country.

Much of your initial treatment was administered on an outpatient basis. But, when you relapsed, your hospital stays became more frequent, and more prolonged. Late in the hot days of August, I visited you in the pediatric intensive care unit. It was your sixteenth birthday—the second time you had spent your birthday in the hospital.

I gave you a copy of Rilke's *Letters to a Young Poet*. I knew that you had many unexpressed feelings, and I thought you might find solace in the deeper dimensions of a poet's views on life. The book is comprised of ten letters that were published posthumously, each letter an answer to an existential question about love, life, and acceptance. Day after day you lay reading that book. As you read, you smiled, for you found recognition and support in the wisdom of Rilke's prose. I saw an awareness in your eyes that finally someone understood how you felt. You told me that Rilke's eighth letter was your favorite. It was about solitude and fear, and appropriately entitled "The Dragon Princess." In this passage, you felt that Rilke was speaking directly to you:

> We have no reason to mistrust our world, for it is not against us. Has it terrors, they are *our* terrors; has it abysses, those abysses belong to us; are dangers at hand, we must try to love them. . . . How should we be able to forget those ancient myths that are at the beginning of all peoples, the myths about dragons that at the last moment turn into princesses; perhaps all the dragons of our lives are princesses who are only waiting to see us once beautiful and brave. Perhaps everything terrible is in its deepest being something helpless that wants help from us.

Looking back I now realize how frightened you were, and how, through the loving and wise words of another poet, you struggled to befriend your fate. You were aware, Julio, that the arc of your life had been revealed, and that the sun was setting before you. What must it have felt like to wrestle with your dragons? To know, and not to know that your fate, in the form of cancer, was asking for help? Your days were filled with questions, struggles, and uncertainty. Looking back, I am amazed again by your resolve, for I see now how determined you were to understand and accept the approach of your mortality.

When your mother learned what the doctors had known for some time, that you would not be able to get back into remission, she came to me with a heavy heart and a broken spirit.

"I don't know what to tell him. I don't know if he knows," she cried.

"What was he told?" I asked.

"The doctors are debating what treatments to give him. I really don't want the doctor to slip and spill the beans. Julio has so much hope, and I really don't want to ruin that. Maybe there's a miracle, you know? But really, there's nothing in sight. I feel that if I tell him the truth he'll give up hope and die quicker. I don't want to bring him down. But I don't want to lie to him either."

"What has Julio been told medically?" I asked.

"He was told that if we try the hospital in the city, there's no guarantee it will work. Only one patient went into remission there. I think all it will do is make things worse for him. I don't want him to suffer anymore. I'm afraid. Julio is smart. He's going to figure it out. "

I sat quietly with your mother, not providing an answer to her unspoken question. What I thought or believed would not help her at that moment; your mother was on a path toward her own awareness and acceptance. We sat quietly, each in our own separate space, thinking about you and how fragile your future was. How does a mother prepare to say goodbye to her child? Slowly, finally, your mother's answer came.

"Just make him comfortable," she said.

I came to your bedside right after that discussion. It was on a Friday, early in the evening, and I knew it would be a long, quiet weekend. The doctors had left their on-call numbers on your nightstand and had gently said their goodbyes.

I remember how I stood there wondering how you would pass the time during the weekend ahead. I thought about my conversation with your mother—how she had struggled to know what was in your heart. She needed to know that you were aware of your fate but could not speak with you about it directly. Your mother was unaccustomed to honest dialogues with her little boy and did not know how to reach you.

In my hand I held a volume of Rilke's collected works, *Ahead of All Parting*, edited and translated by Stephen Mitchell. I believed that you and I could talk through poetry and metaphor. I understood that a dialogue as difficult as this would be best guided through the wisdom of someone outside our relationship. I asked you to read through the book over the weekend and to choose the poem from it that spoke most directly to your heart. I would read my own copy of the book as well, and on Monday we would meet again to exchange our thoughts.

On Monday morning I arrived to discover that you had read every single page of that book, every poem, every word. How you held fast to Rilke's prose; his descriptions of a world of angels, laments, and love. You told me that, after long deliberation, you had chosen your favorite, a poem about wonder, childhood, and contradictions. I asked you to show it to me, and, sitting up straight in your bed as if it were your stage, you began to read aloud:

> As once the winged energy of delight
> carried you over childhood's dark abysses,
> now beyond your own life build the great
> arch of unimagined bridges.

> Wonders happen if we can succeed
> in passing through the harshest danger;
> but only in a bright and purely granted
> achievement can we realize the wonder.

To work with Things in the indescribable
relationship is not too hard for us;
the pattern grows more intricate and subtle,
and being swept along is not enough.

Take your practiced powers and stretch them out
until they span the chasm between two
contradictions . . . For the god
wants to know himself in you.

Here you made your statement, Julio. You spoke about your death, your knowledge of it, and your resolve to conquer it. And you did it eloquently and without ever speaking directly about yourself or your cancer.

"Tell me, Julio, what do you think Rilke means by this poem? What does he mean by 'the great arch of unimagined bridges'?"

"Well," you answered, "it's like stretching this sadness and fear I have into a bridge that will get me to the other side where health remains."

"And what does this statement mean?" I asked. "'Wonders happen if we can succeed in passing through the harshest danger.'"

"I am facing the harshest danger," you explained. "No one believes in a cure. But I am waiting for the wonder. The wonder is the miracle."

"'But only in a bright and purely granted achievement can we realize the wonder.' What is Rilke saying to you here?"

"The achievement is strength and endurance and hope," you answered. "No, not hope. That's a different thing. But my strength will keep me alive."

"And tell me, what is meant by the words, 'And being swept along is not enough'?"

"I want to be in control of my life," you cried. "I don't want to just coast along in life, like a balloon that is swept into the sky, endlessly bumping into clouds and being hit by mountains. I'm like the hand that holds the string and pulls the balloon down."

You were a poet, Julio, but as you spoke, your words moved out of metaphor and into the painful light of reality.

"Tell me then, what is Rilke asserting when he says, 'Stretch them out until they span the chasm between two contradictions'?"

"Well you see," you quietly explained, "everyone says that there is little hope. My mother cries when she looks at me, and the doctors look so sad. This is a place of healing, a hospital, but my healing is taking so long. These are the contradictions. And I want to stretch the energy I have, the 'winged energy of childhood,' into an arch, like an arch of unimagined . . ."

"Unimagined happiness?" I asked you.

"Exactly. That's exactly what I mean!"

"It sounds like you are standing in a field of despair, Julio, and no one sees the arch of unimagined happiness that you see," I added.

"How did you read my mind?" you asked me.

"I'm merely hearing what you've said, Julio," I said. I had finally realized that you understood that this world was not against you. You had befriended your fear and had no reason to mistrust it.

"Tell me, Julio, what is it like underneath the arch?"

"What do you mean?"

"If you could cross the arch of unimagined happiness, where would you find yourself? What would this place be like?" I asked.

"Well, it would be beautiful. It *will* be beautiful. First, my mother will be a successful fund-raiser. She will quit her current job and work full time as a chairperson of her own fund-raising committee and find money to save the lives of other kids like me. And she will be fulfilled and happy in what she does.

"Second, my sister Carmen will be done with college and she will be writing books and she will be happy."

"And you, Julio, what will you be like?"

"Well, I won't have cancer anymore."

"Where will the cancer go?"

"It'll be like the balloon swept away in the sky. And I'll let go of that string."

Then you laughed and offered your thoughts about a life beyond the one you knew.

"I'll be rich," you said. "I'll make a lot of money, and I'll use the money to open a clinic to save the lives of kids who are sick. And they'll always be smiling in my clinic."

"Kind of like Willy Wonka," I said. "Willy Wonka and the healing factory."

"I like that," you smiled. "That's what I'll do under the arch of unimagined happiness."

We sat in silence for a while, dreaming of happiness, chocolate, and restored health. And as we sat, I smiled because I realized that you understood what Rilke was saying. You knew that the dangers at hand were *your* dangers; that what was most terrible in you was, in its deepest dimension, merely asking to be loved. In this way you wrestled with your fate and learned to accept it.

"How do you do it, Julio? How do you remain happy in the face of so much harshness?"

"I have to," you replied. "I have to hope. If I didn't have hope, I couldn't stay alive. As Rilke says, 'If drinking is bitter, turn yourself to wine.'"

"Do you sense that others around you have given up hope?" I asked.

"Yes."

"Who?"

"Well, Dr. B. told me there is nothing else he can do to help me. And he looked so sad. I had to tell him not to worry, not to feel so bad. And when my mother talks to other people, they convince her there is no hope. I see it in her eyes when she looks at me and cries and tells me how sorry she is. And I have to give *her* strength and courage. And I say, 'It's okay, Mom. It won't end! I'm gonna fight this thing.' And she believes me."

I carefully approached your mother. I told her, word for word, about our conversation. I repeated your words, your views on life, death, and acceptance. I read your favorite poem to her and told her what you thought Rilke was saying to you. We sat together for a while, and she cried as she realized that you were aware of your situation. Struck by the depth of your understanding, your mother grew and learned in your last days. She was proud of you. She told everyone she met that her son was a poet.

As she had not in the preceding weeks, your mother sat by your hospital bed every day after our discussion. She asked you to read Rilke's poem of "unimagined happiness" to her. And when you grew too weak to read to her, she softly read to you: "Now beyond your own life build the great arch of unimagined bridges. . . . For the god wants to know himself in you."

You died on a quiet Saturday morning. Your mother and grandmother were not in the hospital at the moment, but you were not alone—you were surrounded by nurses, doctors, and, as your mother believed, God. I wanted to believe that Rilke was there too, guiding you through the land of laments and angels, guiding you home.

Your mother arrived shortly thereafter. She could be heard crying as she was carried through the halls of that sad hospital ward. Her aging father held her under one arm and her mother, your Grandma Rosa, supported her under the other. With each step she wept louder and louder until she saw you, and fell upon your body, and called out your name.

It has been years since your death. Perhaps Rilke was right—that all our dragons are really princesses in disguise, waiting to be embraced. Perhaps there are lessons in the mythical world of childhood where wounds are healed with a mother's kiss. But the world we live in, Julio, isn't inhabited by magical fairies, and our pain is sometimes so severe that it chokes the sputtering flame of hope. But in befriending our fears and in wrestling with sorrows the lesson of surviving them is revealed: that life after a death is not so much about rediscovering joy as it is about the loving acceptance of fate no matter how painful and unjust.

↶ POSTSCRIPT

In our search for acceptance, we develop attachments to the things that the world has to offer. We strive for material wealth, financial success, and physical comfort. We also become attached to our emotions: we wish for moments of joy; we long for love; we ask for mercy. As we age, we become more aware of our mortality. When we are frail and infirm, we pray for strength; when we are lost, we search for meaning; and when we are scared, we seek protection from the injustice of death. It has been said that, like dew from morning grass, what has been ours in life will one day evaporate into the air. What we take with us are not the things we tried so hard to acquire but the essence of lessons learned over time. And we hope that traces of our essence remain after us.

As mortal beings, we are certain that our journey ends in death. Knowing this makes some of us more grateful as the days pass. We appreciate the times when we have been spared pain; we are thankful that someone is listening; and we pray that better days will come. Others face their mortality with bitterness, anxiety, and fear. They rail against the inevitable, question their beliefs in God and an orderly cosmos, and wait anxiously for "the other shoe to drop." How, then, do we acquire the ability to accept our fate? And how do we, as mourners, accept the inevitable when it happens to the ones we love?

Julio's story of pain and transcendence may provide us with an answer, for he faced the reality of his own death in the presence of a loving family of listeners. The medical and the psychosocial staffs devoted time and attention to the emotional as well as the physical aspects of his care. When one member of the medical team was unsure about how to talk and listen to Julio, someone from the psychosocial team was there to help. We learn from Julio that when a story is being told, a true listener is required. Those of us who are less able to understand the symbolism in the words being spoken must be free to defer to someone who is—a pastor, a rabbi, a psychologist, perhaps even a friend.

In bearing witness to our pain, a true listener aids us in our journey toward acceptance. Our need to be taken seriously, to be understood and responded to, is central to our growth. When others bear witness to our inner world, they acknowledge and affirm our importance. Without this acknowledgment, we remain sealed up in solitude. Indeed, what does *not* get heard may drive us further away from the world in which we live and away from our own truer selves. But when our fears and forbidden desires are met with love and understanding, we are able to move beyond the present moment and into a place of greater peace.

Our journey is not a straight or an easy one, however. We are confronted with a myriad of memories, both good and bad. We are reminded of days when our loved one was healthy and vibrant; and we are assaulted by flashbacks of days of suffering and pain. Some of us feel compelled to focus on memories of those darker days. We look compulsively at pictures of our loved ones when they were weak and frail, undergoing medical treatment, or suffering the pain of metastasizing disease. We watch videos or home movies that suddenly remind us of how sick our beloved really was. Or we read and reread news announcements and obituaries of his or her death. These repetitive acts validate our pain and offer an answer to the unrelenting question, "Why isn't he here?" As one mourner put it:

> My husband doesn't understand why I won't throw away the photos taken of our son in his hospital bed. But I can't. I need to look at them again and again. You see, when I look around my house and realize that he is not here, I ask myself, "Where did he go? How is it possible that only a few months ago he was so healthy and so alive, and now he is gone?" And then I look at these pictures and I realize that he had to go. He could not stay here with us any longer, no matter how much I wanted him to.

In searching for acceptance, our memories, whether flashbacks, intrusive thoughts, or moments of deliberate reverie, have another function. They serve as the bridge between the person we used to be and the person life now asks us to become. Our memories anchor us and keep us whole as we struggle to remold a life without our loved one. And as we "remold," we learn to ascribe new meanings to words like acceptance, and strength, and peace. In fact, when we look up "acceptance" in Webster's, we find the following definition: "To receive willingly; to endure without protest; to regard as proper, normal or inevitable; to recognize as true."

The only part of this definition that applies to most mourners is the last; as rational beings we know that we must recognize the truth that our loved one will never return. But the very idea that we accept a loss without complaint may actually make some of us feel angry or hopeless, especially when our loss is "out of order," as in the death of a child. For many, the word "resignation" feels more appropriate. To resign is to give ourselves over without resistance. In essence, we surrender to the grief. As one mother observed:

> Resignation seems, for me, to be a healthier place, especially because it comes with no strings attached. When I surrender, I allow all feelings to come in and wash over me. I welcome both the days I cannot function and the days I feel my life is sweet. The visual I have is of a dog who rolls over on its back and shows its belly, exposing the most vulnerable part of its body in the hope that the aggressor will somehow become its friend. This is the state I live in.

Regardless of how we define it, our struggle to reach a place of acceptance—through surrender, protest, faith, or understanding—remains our eventual goal. It eludes us but keeps us going, day after day. If we are successful in our quest, we discover that, unlike the tidal wave that once carried us under, our grief is now more like a spindrift of tears; we may still see the world through a haze of pain and sadness, but the future, and our place in it, comes back into view. We have faced what we fear most in this life and made ourselves vulnerable to its power. We have wrestled with our sorrow and tried to befriend it. And in the end, we are left with the realization that what is most terrible is, at its deepest core, ours to honor and to own, until it is *our* time to say goodbye.

On Writing the Letters

The Angel Letters was created as a gift of love to the children with whom I worked throughout fifteen years as a psychologist in a pediatric oncology center in New York. It was first conceived as a tribute to friends who, in their short time on earth, taught me gracefully about dying and about the importance of saying goodbye. But *The Angel Letters* was also designed as a means for me as a therapist and friend to these young patients to say my own goodbyes in ways that were honest, uncompromised, and complete. Specifically I found that my stories were sometimes too painful for friends and relatives to hear, and too intimate to share with just "anyone." So I began to write to the children themselves, imagining as I wrote that each child sat before me in gratitude, and in appreciation of my struggle and sorrow. In the process I discovered that the writing of each letter, and the search for the meaning in each life story, helped fortify me through the weeks and years of my own grief. Each letter took a long time to compose—many tears were shed in my effort to say an honest and meaningful farewell to the children I loved. In the end I came to a deeper appreciation of the message that each child's death conveyed about living. And I arrived, eventually, in a place of connection to the life that had just passed, brief as it may have been.

My work with dying children and their families has taught me much about the power of connection. We know, for instance, that when a death occurs, a sense of disempowerment and disconnection from others prevails. Recovery is therefore based upon the empowerment of the survivor and his or her reconnection with the world. Reconnection, however, is never easy to achieve, and that is where the writing of letters may help. As survivors of loss, each of us has a story to tell: it may be about the trauma we have endured or a fear we wrestle with; it may be a collection of involuntary flashbacks or unwelcome fantasies of a seemingly empty future. Whatever our story, it needs to be told. It needs to be unearthed, toiled with, and nurtured in a loving and accepting environment. Letter writing thus became, for me, a distinctive practice that evolved out of my own need to "tell my stories."

When story is used as medicine, it is, in the deepest sense, a healing art. We tell our story and write our letters not because we want to but because we must. Our story summons us from within and asks for an audience. And when we are fortunate enough to find the right listener, the right reader of our letters of love and sorrow, we begin the process of healing. For in writing, we learn that our story is unique, rare and special. The writing and rewriting of our story helps to redefine how we see ourselves. Our words, like our sorrow, become embedded in our hearts; they become a mark upon our soul. And in time we learn to see this mark as our unwitting but faithful companion through time.

The writing of letters and the telling of our story also helps us accept what has happened to us without minimizing our loss. It is an intimate exercise that allows us to haul up our deepest sorrow without having to hear the kind but unhelpful words of hope that well-meaning friends mistakenly offer. It is a personal and often primitive process in which our imagined reader is the beloved family member who died, a wise and knowing peer, a fellow mourner, or simply ourselves. Telling our story in this manner offers us the boundless landscape of the empty page and the hope that, as it is filled, lessons for the living will be learned.

We learn that the very act of living indisposes us to death. Unless confronted with loss or tragedy, most of us go about our days unaffected and unaware, grateful that the tragedies we hear about are happening to someone else, somewhere else. Eventually, and without preparation, we find ourselves ushered into a world of sorrow. But in time we also discover ways to live in this new world. We speak of hope and renewed strength. We see how fragile life is, and we take each other more seriously than we used to.

We learn that the way we die can teach our loved ones how to live. In particular, we discover that only truth confers dignity on end of life.

We discover that women grieve differently than men, and that children understand and experience grief in a wholly different way. Indeed, we learn that children speak a secret, symbolic language when talking about their grief; and we teach ourselves new ways to talk to our children when direct language is too challenging. Further, we discover that old friends rarely understand the journey we are on, while strangers in similar situations can be true kindred spirits.

We learn that love can heal a soul when medicine can no longer heal a body. In time we find ourselves loving again. We discover that allowing new love in our lives is our way of paying homage to the miracle of the love we once had. We learn that, as Galway Kinnell says, "The need for new love *is* faithfulness to the old."

We learn that as time carries us farther away from our trauma, we are transformed. We have seen loved ones and friends "go on" with their lives while we, as mourners, have felt caught in memories of years gone by. We have been surprisingly moved by milestones or by holidays on which we experienced the competing emotions of celebration and secret sorrow. But in time we experience a new sense of reality. We reengage in the activities of the living, and we speak of increased strength. Once again we find ourselves interested in the mundane and ordinary events happening around us.

In writing *The Angel Letters* my sorrow has found meaning. I wrote these letters as a way of wrestling with the questions that death unearthed for me. And I am fortunate to have found loving readers who have allowed my healing to begin. My struggle for understanding, my search for the lessons that each life story in this book has to teach, have brought me closer to a place of acceptance. I pray that such a place will be achieved by you as well someday.

Index

A NOTE ON THE AUTHOR

Norman J. Fried is director of psychosocial services for the division of pediatric hematology/oncology at Winthrop University Hospital and former director of the Children's Cancer Center at North Shore University Hospital on Long Island, New York. A clinical psychologist with graduate degrees from Emory University, he has also taught in the medical school of New York University, and the graduate school of St. John's University, and has been a fellow in clinical and pediatric psychology at Harvard Medical School. He has a private practice in Manhasset, New York. He is married with three sons and lives in Long Island, New York.